1,000,000 Books

are available to read at

---◆---

www.ForgottenBooks.com

---◆---

Read online
Download PDF
Purchase in print

ISBN 978-1-330-08552-3
PIBN 10022040

This book is a reproduction of an important historical work. Forgotten Books uses state-of-the-art technology to digitally reconstruct the work, preserving the original format whilst repairing imperfections present in the aged copy. In rare cases, an imperfection in the original, such as a blemish or missing page, may be replicated in our edition. We do, however, repair the vast majority of imperfections successfully; any imperfections that remain are intentionally left to preserve the state of such historical works.

English
Français
Deutsche
Italiano
Español
Português

www.forgottenbooks.com

Mythology Photography **Fiction**
Fishing Christianity **Art** Cooking
Essays Buddhism Freemasonry
Medicine **Biology** Music **Ancient**
Egypt Evolution Carpentry Physics
Dance Geology **Mathematics** Fitness
Shakespeare **Folklore** Yoga Marketing
Confidence Immortality Biographies
Poetry **Psychology** Witchcraft
Electronics Chemistry History **Law**
Accounting **Philosophy** Anthropology
Alchemy Drama Quantum Mechanics
Atheism Sexual Health **Ancient History**
Entrepreneurship Languages Sport
Paleontology Needlework Islam
Metaphysics Investment Archaeology
Parenting Statistics Criminology
Motivational

JOTTINGS OF TRAVEL

IN

CHINA AND JAPAN

BY

SIMON ADLER STERN.

PHILADELPHIA:

PORTER & COATES.

1888.

TO

WHARTON BARKER,

THE FOLLOWING PAGES ARE INSCRIBED, AS A TOKEN

OF THE REGARD AND ESTEEM OF

THE AUTHOR.

CONTENTS.

APPENDIX.

EARLY in February, 1887, my friend W. B. called at my office one day and, drawing me aside, said that he wanted me to go to China for him, to represent him in certain business matters in which he was interested. He thought that the trip would take about five months; told me that I would have one or two travelling companions, and that the rest of the party would sail from New York, *via* Suez, and join us at Shanghai.

To one who had never been so far away from home that it would take more than a day to return, an invitation to travel to the antipodes was somewhat startling. I had never been much of a traveller, and now I was called upon to say whether I would leave family, friends and business for a voyage of ten thousand miles or more, to far-off Cathay.

It did not take me long to decide; but after I had promised to go, the idea of doing so lost much of its charm. I could not help changing my point of view and gradually succumbed to an attack of homesickness that was severe enough to induce me to give up the projected trip. Odd as it now seems to me to have had a fit of homesickness before leaving home, it was a serious enough matter at the time. In a day or two it yielded to my own treatment—a simple determination to conquer it—and I firmly resolved that, come what might, I would go. I have had abundant reason, since then, to congratulate myself on that decision, for my travels were rich in delightful experiences, and have given me a store of memories that it will always be a pleasure to recall.

I kept no journal of my wanderings, but wrote fully and frequently to my kin at home. Some of the friends who have, from time to time, read those letters, have asked me to put them in more permanent shape; I willingly yield to the request, although I cannot help fearing that the judgment which prompted it may have been an over-friendly one. If I had the slightest reason to believe that the zest with which I enjoyed all that was so new to me could communicate itself to the readers of these pages, I should ask no better warrant than that for putting my hasty jottings by the way into the printer's hands. S. A. S.

August, 1888.

I. Across the Continent.

NO one can feel the potency of home ties more keenly than I do, and it would seem natural and easy to begin by telling about the parting from the loved ones I left behind me. But after all, there is so much that goes without the saying, and that may as well remain untold. My travels began after I left home, and my story ought to do likewise.

For some days I had been uncertain when I was to start. At first I was to go *via* San Francisco, by the S. S. *Belgic*, leaving for Yokohama on the 2d of April. After that, we found that we would have to delay our departure long enough to take passage by the S. S. *City of Peking*, on the 12th. It was, however, out of our power to arrange matters in time, and it was finally decided

that we would go by the S. S. *San Pablo,*
which was advertised to start on the
26th. Uncertain as I was, I had taken
leave of a number of my acquaintances
who when they met me, days and even
weeks afterward, would exclaim, "Oh! I
thought you were half way to China by
this time," with an air that seemed to
imply resentment at my continued.pres-
ence in Philadelphia. I, too, came to
feel that I was lagging superfluous on
the scene, for I had, for the time, so arranged my business as to enable me to
be absent six months or longer, and felt
awkward about taking up my work again
when I could not know at what moment
I might have to drop it.

Finally, on the 9th of April, at about
four o'clock in the afternoon, I became
certain that I would be able to leave
that night. My trunks had been packed
for some days before that. I hurriedly
procured my tickets, called on several
friends to whom I bade hasty *adieux,* and

at 9.50 P. M. left Broad St. Station on the Pacific Express, intending to spend Sunday at Allegheny. Quite a little party had accompanied me to the Station, and when I said good-bye to them it was with a sense of gratitude for their friendly affection rather than of regret at the idea of leaving home. Indeed, I may as well mention it here, I had no further attack of homesickness. The first and only one had been severe enough, and yet I had recovered from it; which fact would have enabled me to bear a relapse with equanimity.

When I alighted from the train at Pittsburgh, the next morning, I found my brother William waiting for me at the railway station. Half an hour later we were in Allegheny, at my sister's pleasant home, discussing, besides all sorts of other congenial topics, a bounteous breakfast.

I left Pittsburgh the same evening at 7.45 and reached Chicago at 9 A. M. of the next day, April 11th. While still **on** the train I noticed in one of the **sub**urbs the following sign, which I thought worth remembering:

Billy Rogers Wabash House.
Oysters & Meals at all Hours.
The Resort of Sports and the Hungry,
The Dry and the Tired.

While walking the busy streets of bustling Chicago, I chanced across Theodore Thomas, who intended to leave that night for Omaha, there to join the National Opera Company. As this was my first visit to Chicago, I found much to interest me in its huge business buildings and **the** active, energetic ways of its people. If I were to put the impression it made upon me into words, I could best describe **it as** a giant that **has** not done growing.

Palace Hotel,

San Francisco, April 19, 1887.

* * * * * I had thought, after leaving Denver, that I would give up correspondence until I had reached the end of my railroad travelling on this Continent, but, in spite of the inconvenience that is inseparably connected with the effort to write while on a rapidly moving railroad car, there was the constant temptation to send a few words to some one at home, and sufficient leisure to gratify it. Not that the motion of the cars was any too rapid, for while between Philadelphia and Chicago we made from thirty-five to thirty-eight miles per hour, our average speed after leaving Chicago was between twenty and twenty-two miles per hour.

M. will probably want to look up our route on his railway maps, and if he will take the folders of the C. B. & Q., the D. & R. G., and the C. P. R., he can easily do so. You may not know just what

these initials stand for, but he will. Our
course, after leaving Chicago, lay through
Northern Illinois, with the prairies on
either side of us. There was nothing in
the shape of scenery to interest one.
It was too early to see the beautiful
green carpet that in the course of the
next few weeks will cover those vast
tracts. It was after nightfall when we
crossed the Mississippi River at Bur-
lingtou, Iowa, where we changed to the
Burlington & Missouri River R. R. We
saw very little of the Iowa portion of
our route, because it was not until morning that we reached Red Oak; somewhat later, we crossed the Missouri
River at a place called Pacific Junction,
and thus entered the State of Nebraska.

We traveled all day and all night,
seeing nothing to the right or left but
the interminable prairie, and stopping
now and then at the stations that, as a
rule, looked uninviting. Most of these
are small towns of which you can get a

fair idea without leaving the platform of your car. When a place is so large that you cannot do this, it is safe to assume that the most unpicturesque portion of it is that nearest the railway. The land is chiefly devoted to farming and grazing; neither the busy look nor the populous settlements of the manufacturing districts of the Eastern and the Middle States are to be met with. That there is wealth and prosperity in the West is an old story by this time. It will probably be a long while before its people are called upon to solve the problem as to what is the greatest number of human beings that can subsist and exist on a given space.

On Friday morning, the 15th, we reached Denver. I would have liked to take time to look about, but in order to do so I would have been obliged to remain there until the next day. On reflection, I concluded that it was best to make no stop until reaching San Francisco. At

Denver we took the cars of the Denver &
Rio Grande Western R. R. This is a
narrow gauge road.

Within a few hours after leaving Denver we were in the mountain country,
which was an agreeable relief after our
long journey through the prairies. In
the afternoon we passed through the
Grand Cañon of the Arkansas, the wildest and most picturesque region that I
have ever seen. It would take either
a fool or a genius to attempt to describe
it; as I do not care to figure as the former, and could not counterfeit the latter
even if I wanted to do so, I shall not try.
On the other hand, I shall probably ruin
myself by purchasing all the photo-
graphic views that I can procure, and
you will have a chance to examine them
on my return.

At Marshall's Pass, in my enthusiasm
at the fact of being 10,800 feet above
the sea level, I sent a few words on a
postal card to M. The cars had stopped;

we were in a snow shed. It was as dark as night and the air was full of smoke from the engine. To the surprise of several of our party, we saw at the side of our train what we supposed to be a post-office, and concluded it would be a good notion to mail what we had written, so that our letters and postal cards would bear the post-mark of Marshall's Pass. A moment later, to our great amusement, we discovered that what we had taken to be a post-office was simply the mail car of our own train, which had been divided into two sections that were lying along side of each other.

During the greater part of Saturday, April 16th, we were travelling through what may best be described as a desert. Not a tree, rarely a stream of water, hardly any vegetation other than the stunted sage-brush, but with the snow-capped Rocky Mountains always in sight. At about 4 P. M. we reached the Salt Lake Valley and, after passing Utah

Lake, we came upon a stretch of country showing the results of Mormon thrift. Here we saw grassy meadows, blossoming fruit trees, grazing herds of cattle and flocks of sheep. Salt Lake City, as seen from the station, was rather disappointing. The new Temple and the Tabernacle were pointed out to us; the other buildings seemed insignificant, and the town (or city) had a straggling, scattered look. Leaving Salt Lake City and passing along the border of the Great Salt Lake, we soon reached Ogden, where we changed to the cars of the Central Pacific R. R.

When we awoke on Sunday, we were in Nevada. That whole day was a journey through the desert, with mountains, bluffs and buttes in view all the time. The only incident was that at Battle Mountain Station our train was made to wait while the train carrying the National Opera Company to San Francisco was allowed to pass us. They stopped

long enough to give me a chance to exchange greetings with *Concert-meister* Ben-
dix and a few other acquaintances of mine
who were of the party. While I was
talking to them the train started; by the
time I had rushed out to the platform of
the car it was moving quite rapidly.
Luckily, I jumped off without doing myself any injury and had to walk back
some distance to where our train was
waiting. When I found time to think of
what I had done, I concluded that it
would have been far more prudent to
have remained with the Opera people
until the next station was reached.

At several of the stations in Nevada
we saw numbers of Indians; men, women
and children. They were not very pleasant to behold. Some of them had their
papooses bundled up in the way that
we have often seen in pictures. Most
of them were sitting about in groups,
listless, lazy-looking and unmistakably
dirty. At Winnemucca, a group of

Indian girls, of various complexions, one of them rather light in color and with pleasing features, were playing at ball. They showed themselves graceful and agile enough at that.

We went to sleep while travelling through the Nevada desert, but when we awoke the next morning we were in a garden; for during the night we had crossed the Sierra Nevada, and were at last in California. Green, grassy mountains, fine trees, and all vegetation as far advanced as it would be in our part of the country in June. On the way to San Francisco, I saw bushes covered with thick clusters of lovely roses, calla lilies growing in the gardens, and field flowers in great variety. Especially noticeable, both because of its abundance and its beauty, was a field poppy of a rich dark orange color, which the people hereabouts mis-name "buttercup."

At about noon we reached Oakland, a beautiful suburb of San Francisco, where we took the steamboat that brought us to the city. We have installed ourselves at the Palace Hotel, a huge building, unlike any other hotel I have yet seen, in the fact of its being built around four sides of a court-yard, which is roofed in with glass. Wide galleries on each of the six floors look down into the centre space through which the various offices, the dining-rooms, etc., are reached. We are comfortably quartered here, and this is well, for we are told that our stay in San Francisco will be five days longer than we had expected, as the S. S. *San Pablo's* departure has been postponed from the 21st to the 26th. We learn at the same time, that the S. S. *City of Peking* sailed on the 16th, instead of the 12th. Had we known that, we might have reached here in time to go by that steamer. We indulge in no vain regrets on that account, however, for we are quite willing to believe that a few more days of San Francisco can be profitably and agreeably spent by us.

Last evening we heard one act of *Ruddygore*. We found the dialogue wearisome; yet, for the sake of the music we would gladly have waited to the end. But we were tired, the theatre was cold, and, after our long experience of sleeping-cars, we were somewhat anxious to sleep in a real bed.

II. San Francisco.

Palace Hotel,
San Francisco, April 25, 1887.

* * * * * I mentioned my having been invited to a Chinese dinner, or rather a dinner in a Chinese restaurant, for, in deference to the tastes of the Americans and Europeans in the company, our host, the Chinese Consul-General at this port, had arranged that certain American dishes should be provided; thus, it was, in a sense, an international banquet.

I found it a most enjoyable affair, and felt as if I had already entered the Orient. The dining-room was prettily ornamented with gilt carving of fine workmanship and was separated from a sort of sitting-room by a partition formed of stained glass set in a frame work of ebony and more gilt carving. There were nine of us at dinner. The table was tastefully decorated with flowers, the service was excellent, and the *menu* included such tid-bits as bird's-nest stew, snow fungus (imported from the North of China, and said to be quite costly), sturgeon stew with mushrooms and bamboo shoots, shark's fins with eggs, rice pasty with shrimps, and liche nuts. I made it a point to neglect none of these dishes and can assure you some of them were palatable, and one or two quite delicate. Although knives and forks were provided, I thought it well to take my first lesson in the use of chopsticks, and after a little practice I did fairly well with them.

The Queen of the Sandwich Islands and her suite have been staying at this hotel for some days. She is an amiable looking mulatto woman, about forty-five years of age. In honor of her arrival, the Hawaiian national colors were displayed, and in the evening there was a serenade by the band. She leaves here soon for New York, and proposes to be in London in time for the Queen's Jubilee.

When I speak to Californians of the roses and other flowers that bloom here so much earlier than they do with us, they assure me that the rose bushes are just as full of roses, and the grass as green and plentiful, in January as at present. They go away during the summer because it is damp, foggy and chilly, and seek points in Southern California where it is warm and dry. They grow quite enthusiastic on the subject of California and its climate, and every now and then will tell me, " This is God's own country."

San Francisco is a brisk, bustling sort of city, with quite a cosmopolitan air. To one used to Philadelphia's quiet ways it seems, at first sight, to be about four times as large as it really is. There are several large and excellent hotels, and quite a number of good restaurants. One of these is known by the inviting

name of " The Pup," another is " The
Poodle."   If you value your reputation
for good judgment and politeness, you
must not contradict a San Franciscan
when he tells you that either of these is
at least as good a restaurant as Delmon-
ico's or the Hotel Brunswick.

There are many large business buildings and fine shops of all kinds. Of a
Saturday afternoon, you will find Kear-
ney Street thronged with a crowd dense
enough to remind you of Chestnut Street
or Broadway at their best. The dwellings
are nearly all built of wood, suggesting
the suburban villas of our Eastern cities.
Many of them are ornate in appearance,
and the interiors are often elaborately
finished and lavishly furnished. It is
thought best not to build of brick or
stone; firstly, because of the humid atmosphere during the rainy season, when,
I imagine, things are not so lovely hereabouts as at present; secondly, because
of the danger of earthquakes.

The city is quite hilly and is crossed in different directions by cable cars, which are run here far more satisfactorily than in Philadelphia or Chicago. Whenever you get to **the** top of one of the hills, you have charming views of the beautiful **Bay** and the heights beyond. I shall spare you a description of the Park, the Cliff House, and the Seal Rocks, but shall make up for this by sending you photographs of those points of interest.

The H. family received me with open arms. They have made me so welcome, and have been so kind in their unremitting efforts to make my stay here a pleasant one, that I shall hate to say good-bye to them, for it will seem like leaving home a second time.

III.   On the Pacific.

Yesterday, at 1.45 P. M., our carriage being in waiting, we started for the steamer wharf. The S. S. *City of Sydney*, which had arrived a day or two before, was discharging its cargo. The S. S. *San José* was also lying alongside of the pier, and the busy wharfmen were carrying sacks of coffee ashore.

About a hundred Chinese go with us, as steerage passengers. They were accompanied to the wharf by their friends, who helped to swell the crowd. They were all provided with the proper certificates, allowing them to return to the United States; it is pretty well understood that the certificate always returns to our shores, but rarely in the hands of him to whom it was originally issued. By the time the owner reaches Hong

Kong, it has become an asset with a well-established market price and a ready sale.

The Chinese Consul-General, the Consul (Colonel Bee) and the Secretary of the Consulate came to the steamer to see us off, and to take leave of the two mandarins, attachés of the Chinese Legation at Berlin, who return by the *San Pablo*. In honor of their presence, the yellow flag bearing the device of the dragon was displayed, as well as the Stars and Stripes. Several gentlemen whose acquaintance we made on the train or in San Francisco have joined the few friends who have come to say good-bye. They are, one and all, so pleased with the looks of the vessel that they say they would like to take the trip with us.

The hour announced for our departure was 2 P. M. At about half-past one o'clock we were informed that the mail train from the East was two hours late, and that we would be delayed accordingly. At a few minutes before four o'clock the gang plank was drawn ashore and we started on our long voyage. A moment later the surface of the water in the dock was covered with bits of paper of divers colors and sizes, which had been thrown overboard by our Chinese steerage passengers, as offerings to propitiate the water-god. What is to be seen while sailing down the beautiful Bay of San Francisco and through the Golden Gate is so happily described in the little book with which we all made ourselves so familiar while I was yet at home, that I need not write a word about it. The broad waters beneath us; craft of many kinds, large and small, around and about us; with the verdure clad hills encircling the Bay, for a background: formed a picture that I shall long remember.

In the course of about two hours we were out at sea; to use the sailors' expression, the water was rather " humpy," and the wind, blowing strongly from the West, was against us. The vessel pitched considerably and rolled a little. At about half-past six o'clock the gong summoned us to dinner. Out of the twenty or more saloon passengers, some seven or eight put in an appearance, and of the ladies, none were to be seen. It was rough all evening. At about ten o'clock, after a pleasant chat in the smoking-room with the Captain, the Purser and a Mr. M., a tea and silk merchant on his way to Yokohama, I retired. The Captain asked me how I was standing it. I told him that I was feeling quite comfortable; whereupon he remarked, that if I could stand that, there was little likelihood of my getting sea-sick.

Grand Hotel,

Yokohama, May 17, 1887.

In the letter that I began while on shipboard, and which I dated April 27th, the day after we started, I told you about our last hours in San Francisco and our first experiences at sea. As I have had no chance until now to mail what was then written, it will go to you with this.

The S. S. *San Pablo* was originally intended for a coaler, to ply between San Francisco and Tacoma, but was chartered by the O. & O. Co. and placed on their line. As there were accommodations for only six or eight first-class passengers, she was re-fitted for the regular passenger traffic by the Union Foundry Company of San Francisco. A new deck was added, with twenty or more staterooms, and arrangements made to aecommodate a considerable number of second-class and steerage passengers. I had made the acquaintance of Captain Reed, the officer commanding the *San Pablo*, while in San Francisco, having brought a letter of introduction from the builders of the vessel, Messrs. Cramp, of Philadelphia.

This was the first trip made by the *San Pablo* after being thus refitted.

We passed several ships on the day after we left port. After that, not a sail was seen until, on the morning of May 15th, we were steaming up the Bay of Yokohama.

During the long voyage we were favored with pleasant weather until the last day. We took the course along the 37th parallel of north latitude until nearing the coast of Japan. Our sails, however, were of no use, as, during the greater part of the time, we had head winds. The steamers that cross the Pacific are not to be hurried, and the Captains are expected to be sparing of the coal used. The *San Pablo's* allowance was about forty tons per day.

The voyage was a leisurely one. Looking forward to it, it seemed very long; looking back, it was so void of incident, in its pleasant monotony, as to seem very short. Still, it was an important event in my life. My first sea voyage, so to say, for I had never before that been at sea more than a day and a night. I thoroughly enjoyed it, for I was so fortunate as not to have one moment of sea-sickness. I attempted to read, but read very little; I smoked, lounged about, chatted with my fellow-passengers, bored myself at whist, or joined in the few games on deck for the sake of the exercise they afforded. It was a never-ending delight to watch the ocean, at one time " deeply, darkly, beautifully blue," at another gray, then green, then of a dull leaden color, almost black; now almost as smooth as a mill-pond, except for the long swell with which our vessel would slowly rise and then as gently sink again, and at other seasons playful or angry by turns.

Late on Friday, May 6th, we crossed the line (the 180th meridian) and lost a day, leaving Saturday out of that week. Vessels going East gain a day at this point and thus take up what has been lost. If there be less travelling in one direction than in the other, there must be a number of dropped days there waiting for some one to take them in and make use of them.

One advantage of travelling by water instead of on land is that you save the expense of a linen duster. Unfortunately, however, while you escape the dust, you cannot, unless you go by sailing vessel, so easily avoid the cinders. One got lodged in my eye and gave me much pain for several days, until I called on the ship's doctor for relief. With the aid of an instrument, he removed it, but the eye had become so inflamed that it required treatment for some days afterward.

Our diversions were of the mildest. One day we were all invited to a "four o'clock tea," our hostess being a Mrs. T., wife of a prosperous tea merchant of Yokohama and Kobé. As she said she must have some one to "bring out" on the occasion, she pitched upon Mr. M., a

portly, middle-aged gentleman, as her *deb-
utant*. We had tea galore, with singing
and guitar playing, and the tea was much
better than the music. One of our Chinese friends played on a Chinese flute
and afterward sàng some Chinese comic
songs, which were quite caterwaulish. All
of the saloon passengers had been invited
and none sent regrets. It was considered
a pleasant break in the day, and, for that
matter, in the trip. We had been at sea
for fourteen or fifteen days. After so long
a voyage, the most enthusiastic lover of
old ocean must, I opine, be glad to hear
the words: " Land ahead!"

There was much sociability among the
passengers. Introductions were unneces-
sary. I have renewed acquaintance with
many old anecdotes and had the great
good luck of getting rid of some of my
old ones, *at par*.

On the 14th of May, the last day out, we
had a stiff gale with a heavy rain-storm.
It began in the morning and lasted until

nightfall, leaving the sky black and the sea very rough. In the opinion of the Captain and the First Officer, the velocity of the wind was between seventy and eighty miles per hour. When it was all over, they told us that we had passed through a severe and dangerous storm, and that it had blown strongly enough for a typhoon. In my ignorance, I was not aware of the danger, but quite sensible of the discomfort, for the vessel pitched and rolled so violently as to make it difficult to move about without holding on to something. I had managed to make my way along the slippery deck, from the smoking-room to the door of the saloon, and was about to step inside, when the vessel gave a sudden lurch that sent me flying in the other direction, until the rail stopped me from going any further. When I got up I was, with the exception of a few scratches, none the worse for my fall. At dinner it required skilful management to prevent your soup from travelling across table, and the only way to avoid having your wine spilled was to drink it off as soon as it was poured out. I did not mind the discomfort, but gave up almost the entire day to watching the huge waves that would now and then dash over the roof of the saloon and the smoking-room. I was gratified at beholding the storm and at being in it, and yet my curiosity in that direction was so fully satisfied by that day's experience, that, instead of wishing for a worse, I trust I may never again be in so violent a one. I was not afraid, except as realizing that one is always in danger while on the water. While I knew that, for the time being, our risk was increased, I had enough confidence in the ship's officers not to worry.

On the next morning, May 15th, I awoke at about half-past four o'clock. Looking out of my port window, I saw that the sun was shining brightly and that two fishing junks were passing us, .

outward bound. It did not take me long to dress and hurry on deck, where I found most of the passengers already assembled. We were steaming up Yokohama Bay. On either side of us were the green shores of Japan, and Fujiama (i. e. the peerless mountain), snow-capped and in majestic beauty, was plainly seen, although about seventy miles distant. The blue water, the glorious sky, the pretty gardens, the brilliant verdure, the odd-looking bungalows, the queerly-built craft in the shape of junks and sampans, with their swarthy, sinewy, half-naked crews—all combined to make a scene that I shall never forget. All seemed so new, so strange, so beautiful, that in my enthusiasm I felt it would have been worth making the journey of some eight thousand miles, if only for the sake of experiencing the delights of that joyous entry into Japan.

It was about eight o'clock in the morning when we dropped anchor before

Yokohama, and a little while later the crowd of sampans that we had seen coming out to meet us drew up alongside of the *San Pablo*.* Boatmen and runners were soon jostling each other in the effort to be first on the companion ladder that led to the steerage, for their business lay chiefly in that quarter. In the meanwhile, small steam launches had arrived; one to carry away the mails, another in the service of the steamer company, and still another from the Grand Hotel. We embarked on this, gladly giving up the chance of another breakfast on the *San Pablo* for the sake of once more enjoying a meal on land. In less than ten minutes from that time I stepped ashore at the English *hatoba* (landing place), paid my respects to the polite custom-house officers, jumped

---

*See Appendix, under the caption "Chinese Pirates," for an account of the wreck of the ill-fated *San Pablo*.

into a *jin-ricsha* (the one-man phaeton which is the principal vehicle in this country), and was hurried along the Bund to the Grand Hotel.

IV. YOKOHAMA.

Yokohama, May 17, 1887.

* * * * In the two days that have
passed since my arrival I have seen much
of Yokohama, and my appetite for sight-
seeing seems to grow with every hour.

Our friends have gone to the races.
This is a sort of holiday with the foreign population of Yokohama. As it is
an English or American, rather than
a Japanese institution, I shall, instead
of going to the grounds, devote this afternoon to letter writing.

We are very comfortably fixed at the
Grand Hotel. If the dining-room is not
a Babel in the way of noise, it is one so
far as a "confusion of tongues" can go
to make it so. It seems to be a gathering
place for specimens (not always of the

choicest) of all sorts of nationalities; for
you can meet Americans, Englishmen,
Frenchmen, Germans, Dutch, Spaniards,
Russians, Hindoos and even Armenians
there. The servants are Japanese, the
steward is a Chinaman who speaks excellent French, the clerk in charge of the
office is Portuguese, the *comprador* is of
course a Chinaman and, if I remember
rightly, the night watchman is a Wallachian.

As it has been deemed advisable to de-
fer going to China until we have called
on some of the Japanese gentlemen to
whom we bear letters of introduction,
we have postponed our departure for
Shanghai for at least a week. Our original plan was to go to-day.

To-morrow, we hope to visit Tokio, the
capital, and, from what I have heard,
we are likely to find the old city even
more interesting than Yokohama.

You have probably read so much about
the Japanese booths (one-story wooden

structures, with the whole front opening on the sidewalk), and have seen so many pictures of these low buildings with their odd-looking tile roofs, that you know what they are without any description of mine. The real enjoyment is to see whole streets of them; to see the tailor, the butcher, the sandal-maker and the fish merchant plying their various trades; to see the wilderness of babies, for they are met with at every turn, of all sorts and sizes and in appalling profusion; and then, again, to pass through the same streets after nightfall, when colored paper lanterns are hung up in front of every booth.

The last letter I received from home reached me on the day I left San Francisco, April 26th. If at Shanghai I can intercept any letters for me that may be on their way to Pekin, I shall try to do so. But even in that case I shall have to wait until, say, a fortnight hence, thus making it some five weeks, or more, between letters. A long time, truly. I trust that they may bring me good news from all of you.

* * * * * ← *

Our hotel is delightfully situated on the Bund, the name by which the high-way along the water front is designated in these Eastern cities. It affords a fine view of the beautiful Bay, which has a peaceful, quiet look, but which, I am told, can be very turbulent, and often is so, at very short notice.

The evenings in such a place are, as a rule, very quiet. Sometimes, late at night, when all the guests have retired, I find it pleasant enough to light a cigar and take my seat on the veranda. The Wallachian watchman, going his rounds, will stop for a minute's chat, and then will leave me to myself and my thoughts of what the day has brought and taught me, of the people I have met, of the sights I have seen, and of the friends at home. The silence is broken at intervals by the passing of a group of *jin-ricshas,* conveying their passengers homeward from some festive gathering, the spell of which is still evident in the noisy gayety of the merry riders.

Then, too, there is the shampooer or rubber, usually a blind man, who wanders the streets at night seeking employment, and obtaining it, too. He carries a little fife or flute, on which he sounds two notes, an ascending fifth, so that those who are weary and yet unable to sleep may know of his coming. His fees are ridiculously low when compared with those of our artists in *massage*, although I am told his work is equally as good as theirs.

But, for that matter, the wages of native laborers are said to range between 20 and 30 *sen* per day. The *sen* equals about four-fifths of an American cent. These are city wages; in the country districts they are even lower. This opens up a subject on which I am tempted to enlarge, but I am afraid of wearying you ; and, putting the better reason last, I am not, as yet, sufficiently familiar with economic conditions hereabouts to feel like hazarding a judgment upon them.

From what I have seen and heard thus far, I should conclude that, while there are a few rich Japanese, the average of wealth is quite low. On the other hand, it would seem that the masses are content with their condition, and their simple wants such as are easily gratified, even with the pittance their daily toil ensures them.

These remarks do not, however, apply to what may be called Young Japan, that large and growing section of the population that has eagerly welcomed Western methods, and that, in science, law, commerce and finance has done so much for Japanese progress. When I use the word *large* in this connection, I have in view the character and influence of the people forming this class, rather than their numbers. The Japanese have shown great powers of adaptation in taking up foreign ideas, and very considerable skill in carrying them out. Their telegraph service is an excellent one; the post-office is equally efficient; their system of national banks and their decimal currency are based on American methods, indeed, but they have been before us in establishing postal savings banks.

But enough of this for to-day. One of my ways of passing my time here is to write letters. The reading will not take as long as the writing of them, and yet they may weary you if I dwell too long on such serious topics. Indeed, I have more than once imagined you asking yourself: " Do all people who take their first journey have this tiresome way of assuming that nobody else has ever been anywhere ? "

V. Yokohama–Tokio.

Yokohama, May 18, 1887.

We left the hotel at about 9 o'clock this morning, and, seated in *jin-ricshas*, were soon hurrying along the Bund; thence, through one of the cross streets, or rather lanes, lined on either side with *go-downs*, low, one-story warehouses, devoted to tea-firing and other commercial uses, into Main Street, where the Hong Kong and Shanghai Banking Corporation and other financial institutions have their offices. Leaving Main Street, we entered the Honcho-dori, where some of the best shops for curios, pottery, bronzes, silks and lacquer ware are to be found, and after two or three more turns we at last alighted at the railway station, a large building of brick and stone. On entering, we met a crowd of Japanese, who had just alighted from an arriving train, and whose wooden sandals made quite a clatter on the asphalt pavement. Everything in and about the station betokened neatness and careful management. The narrow-gauge tracks (the rails three feet apart), the small cars, and the diminutive-looking engines, suggested a railway in miniature. The coaches are arranged for three classes of passengers. The first, with their soft, cushioned seats, are warm, stuffy and expensive; the second are quite comfortable and are used indiscriminately by foreigners and natives; the third have simple wooden benches; as a rule, these carry only Japanese passengers, and at a very low price.

The railway from Yokohama to Tokio is only eighteen miles in length and the trip lasts about forty-five minutes. The first station is Kanagawa, which, although an older settlement, is, in effect, a suburb of Yokohama, which has grown out towards it. On the left there are pretty hills for some distance along the route; on the right, the Bay. We pass numbers of paddy-fields, in which we see natives working in the mud, into which they have sunk so deep that only the upper portion of their bodies is visible. It looks like dirty work, and one might search far and wide to find a more unclean-looking set of husbandmen. We are told, however, that every one of these laborers will cleanse himself in a hot bath when the day's work is done. If report speaks truly, the Japanese are a nation of bathers. The "daily tub" is a national institution; and that they think a bath must be a hot one, I have already been taught by my *boy* at the hotel.

As we approach Tokio we see the forts in the Bay and large numbers of freight-laden .junks and lighters bringing merchandise of various kinds from Yokohama. There are no large vessels in these shoal waters, but the smaller craft do quite a profitable business, as the greater portion of the freight is sent up from Yokohama by water, because the rates by railway are almost prohibitory.

The railway does a large passenger business. Trains run in either direction almost hourly, and the company's facilities are taxed to the utmost. Additional tracks will be needed if it is intended to compete with the junks and lighters for the freight traffic. There can, however, hardly be a doubt that it would pay to make the outlay. Perhaps the first cost of the road has frightened the company out of the notion of more track-laying. This, the first railway built in Japan, involved, in proportion to the size of the plant, an enormous outlay. No one seems to know exactly what it did cost, but such figures have been named as make railway engineers shrug their shoulders and wonder where all the money can have gone. Nevertheless, the Japanese may be congratulated on having a pretty little railway, on which the service is excellent. It was the beginning of the railway system in this country. At the present writing there are, I understand, some four hundred miles of railroads in the Empire, with numerous additional lines projected or already under way. The Tokio-Yokohama line was built at government expense, which may in part explain why it cost so much. There is no need of one's travelling so far from home to find similar instances of a lavish use of public funds. The present policy of the government is to encourage the forming of joint stock companies for such purposes, leaving private persons to take the initiative; thus rendering it tolerably certain that future undertakings will be based on the actual needs of the community and will be conducted with proper economy. When credit becomes cheaper, capital more abundant, and speculation rampant, they may still further emulate the example of American railway pro-

moters by paralleling routes, watering
stock, and cutting rates. May such a
season be long deferred. In the meanwhile, however, they might benefit themselves and certain American manufacturers, by giving the latter a chance to
prove the superiority of our locomotives
and railway equipment to those of British manufacture.

The terminus of the road is at Shinbashi Station in Tokio. When we reached
the street we found ourselves in a wilderness of *jin-ricshas*, carts and carriers,
and soon realized that we were in an
older, larger, greater and dirtier city
than the young and clean-looking Yokohama that we had left only a little while
before.

As we wanted to see all that was to be
seen, we thought it better to walk than
to ride, and started for the *Ginza*, the
main thoroughfare of Tokio. It is a wide
street, with shops on either side and tram-
way cars running through the centre.

We walked for a long while, but found the shops less interesting than those of Yokohama. In Tokio the chief business is with Japanese, and the articles dealt in are, for the greater part, such as enter into their daily wants. There are in certain quarters many large establishments devoted entirely to the wholesale trade, and these have a busy, prosperous look. Tourists, who usually confine their purchases to objects of ornament, can find better shops for what they want at Yokohama and, I am told, at Kobé, Kioto and Nagasaki.

After tramping along the hot and dusty *Ginza* for an hour or more, we began to weary of the interminable rows of two-story buildings and the tedious repetition of shops for cigarettes and smoker's articles, for American and European drinks, for hats, dried fish, paper, tea, crockery, baskets, and what not, but our interest in the crowds of foot-passengers and *jin-ricsha* riders was unabated. The cross streets seemed to be just as densely built, and with the end nowhere in sight from the *Ginza ;* although, with one or two exceptions, they were less crowded.

Tokio is said to contain a population of about 1,000,000, and has over 3,000 temples. As few of the houses are more than two stories high, it is easy to understand why it covers so large a space, for its area is about the same as that of London. It seems to be an aggregation of villages which have grown out towards one another until the interspaces have all been filled up, making, as a grand total, the present capital of Japan. These various villages, in most instances, furnish the names of the districts into which the city is divided. In this vast place, there are, all told, about 150 Americans and Europeans.

The Japanese were nearly all in native costume. The greater portion of those who wore the European dress were young men, presumably officials or professors.

Those in Japanese dress, whether male or female, were almost invariably provided with fan, pipe, tobacco-pouch and paper umbrella. Some of the attempts to combine the fashions of the East and the West were both incongruous and amusing.

Two *jin-ricsha* coolies, who had marked us for their own as soon as they **saw** us at the Shinbashi station, had followed us all this time, and had, every few moments, asked us to get in and ride. One of them knew a few words of English and had done us some slight service in our dealings with various shopkeepers on the *Ginza.* He **was** a bright fellow, with an engaging smile, and, like all of his countrymen I have thus far met, polite and obliging.

It was high noon. We were warm, tired and hungry, and, seating ourselves in the *jin-ricshas*, we directed our boys to take us to the Sey-yo-Ken restaurant. After a ride of about a quarter of an hour

we found ourselves within the borders of
the beautiful Uyeno Park, travelling along
a wide, smooth road, under fine old shade
trees, whose foliage sheltered us from the
heat and the glare of the noon-day sun.
Turning to the left, we soon reached the
restaurant to which we had been directed
by mine host Wolf, of the Grand Hotel.
It is kept by Japanese; but, as the meals
are served in the European style, tables
and chairs are provided for the guests.
We thought it well to take our *tiffin*
(luncheon) in the pretty garden, rather
than sit in-doors, and were soon served
with a nicely prepared meal, to which,
after the morning's exertions, we were in
a mood to do full justice.

Seated at one of the tables there was
an elderly Japanese gentleman convers-
ing with a young, florid-looking Englishman. They both used the language of
the country. Although I could not
understand more than a word or two now
and then, I watched the pair with much

interest, for I was attracted by the wise and complacent air of the old man as well as by the fine spirits and healthy appearance of the lusty youth.

We were in no hurry to leave the quiet, peaceful place, and lingered there for some time after luncheon, watching the rooks that were flying about in great numbers. The adjoining bell-tower and the trees were full of them, and their incessant cawing suggested the query whether the rook is the chief singing bird of Japan.

The Park and the temple within its borders both take their name from the district (Uyeno) in which they are situated. As I have been informed that I shall find the temples of Shiba and Asakusa more interesting than that at Uyeno, I shall spare you a description of the latter.

We visited the Exposition building, also in the Park, in which we saw attractive exhibits of Japanese work in enamels, bronzes, pottery, painting, lacquered ware and fans, as well as in such lines as chemicals, builders' hardware, joiners' work, paper-hangings, etc. Among the paintings there were numerous specimens in oil, after the European manner as to perspective and the treatment of color. They left much to be desired, and were vastly inferior to the work in the true Japanese style, the most noteworthy examples of which were the screens.

At one end of the large building, a military band of about fifty performers, all of them natives, were playing a selection from *L'Africaine*, in excellent style. The Japanese crowded about the music pavilion, listening intently, as it seemed, although I could not help wondering whether they think the Western music equal to the caterwaulish strains of their own *gaishas*, and the tum-tum accompaniment of the *samisen* or *koto*. I have asked several Japanese gentlemen who, while pursuing their studies in Europe or America, cultivated a taste for what *nous autres* call music, to enlighten me on this point. In every instance, they told me that, while they prefer "European" music, they are nevertheless swayed by the spell of their own national melodies and the words to which they are set. I can easily believe that part of it, but how they can enjoy both kinds passes my understanding.

But, sooner or later, all things must end, even this long letter. I have nearly got to the end of this sheet and shall not begin another to-night.

Our day had been a tolerably busy one, as you will probably conclude by the time you have read thus far. So, as it was already quite late in the afternoon, we left the Exposition building, jumped into our *jin-ricshas*, and were soon travelling along the *Ginza*, which we found still more thronged than it had been in the morning. Reaching the Shinbashi station, we took the train and returned to Yokohama.

VI. SHIBA.

Since I last wrote you, I have again been in Tokio, the object of my visit being to see the Temple of Shiba, of which you can get a good idea from the excellent photographs I send you by this mail. There are several temples, and it is safe to say they are prettier by far in the nicely-colored sun-pictures than in reality, for, like everything in Tokio, they have a dusty look and would be the better for a coat of paint.

So much for first impressions. In spite of them, I thoroughly enjoyed the hour and a half that I spent roaming about the grounds. The place was impressive because of its death-like silence. Excepting a half-starved looking Japanese youth who followed me at a respectful distance, but whose curiosity would not permit him to take his eyes off of me, I was alone while I trod the pebble pavement, wandered through the darkened groves, or tried to count the many stone lanterns, votive offerings, whose inscriptions were to me illegible and, for that reason, perhaps, the more impressive.

In the temples, I found enough to interest me in the grotesque carvings of the eaves and the heavy portals, in the odd mixture of real art and tawdry ornament on and about the altars, and in the deserted appearance of the buildings, emphasized in this instance by the presence of a solitary priest in the smaller and brighter looking one.   But the impression I brought away with me was due rather to the dismal beauty of the temple grounds.   There are giant trees, whose great trunks and sturdy branches show their age, but whose rich, thick foliage, shutting out the sunlight, prove it to be

a "green old age." I lingered there long
after I had beheld all that was to be seen.

As I am not learned in other péople's
religions, I indulged in no philosophic
reflections on Buddhism or Shinto-ism. I
could not, however, help thinking that
the Shiba temples, in their emptiness,
seemed to say that all who had ever wor-
shipped there had long since emigrated
to the land of spirits. Once upon a time
Shiba was a great shrine, and it is easy
to imagine the vast enclosure thronged
with pilgrims from all parts of Japan,
paying obeisance to Buddhist priests,
rendering homage to the pot-bellied
images, and devoutly tending the lamps
in the stone lanterns. It must have
been a brilliant scene, rich with color
effects and instinct with life and motion.
Whether they beat the *tam-tam* then, as
I heard them beating it outside of one of
the Homura temples the other day, I
cannot say. But of one thing I am sure
—there must have been lots of babies

there, for I never saw a real Japanese crowd without them. Some of the babies that you see during your walks, are really the handsomest creatures in Japan.

If I were attempting to indulge in fine writing, I should consider it quite a happy hit thus to lug in the infants; for the mere mention of them in connection with Shiba, suggests life, where now all is silent as death.

VII. A Fire in Yokohama.

Grand Hotel,

Yokohama, May 24th, 1887.

This is a general holiday among the Europeans and Americans residing here. Business of nearly all kinds is suspended, for it .is Queen Victoria's birthday. Although it is more especially an English holiday, foreigners of all nationalities seem to take part in its observance.

The weather is perfect, the sky is cloudless, except near the opposite shore of lovely Yokohama Bay; the air is soft and balmy, hardly stirring the waters into a ripple. A little while ago, just before I came in-doors, it was a pretty sight to watch the boats carry the American marines and sailors, who assisted in the celebration, back to our vessels of war, the *Brooklyn*, the *Omaha*, the *Palos*, and the *Monocacy*, all of which are stationed here at present. There are also French, English and Russian frigates, as well as merchant steamers of various nationalities, lying at anchor before the town.

When our boys marched past here on their way to the boats it sounded quite natural to hear the band of the *Brooklyn* play "Marching through Georgia." The melody is not a beautiful one, but it reminded me of home, and was enjoyed the more on that account.

I am not in the habit of running to fires in Philadelphia, but I have just witnessed one here, and found much entertainment in the spectacle, although when I got back to the hotel I found that an intaglio that I had worn attached to my watch chain had parted company with me whilst in the crowd.

Shortly after luncheon I went to the Japanese suburban village of Homura, to

make a small purchase. I had finished
my business and was examining some
painted screens which the polite shop-
keeper was showing me, when a young
girl rushed into the shop to inform him
that there was a fire. Without another
word, he left me, hurriedly exchanged his
straw sandals for wooden ones, and
darted down the street. Curious to see
how they order these things in Japan, I
followed him, and was soon one of the
motley crowd that rushed over the bridge
connecting Homura with Yokohama.

The fire was in Chinatown, in the establishment of a shoemaker, opposite to
Mr. Cock-Eye's tailor shop and next door
to Mr. Ah-Why's carpenter shop. It was
a sort of sailors' quarter, and close by
were quite a number of low-looking
places with high sounding titles, such as
*Café de l'Univers, Boulangerie Provençale,
A la descente des Marins,* etc. Chinese
shopkeepers, Japanese men, women and
babies, Chinese and Japanese coolies,

American sailors, and an assorted lot of Europeans, helped to make up the crowd. With the exception of the Germans and Americans who belong to the fire company, all were more or less excited. Japanese policemen, clad in white duck uniforms, were present in large numbers, and were running hither and thither as if bewildered. There were also several Japanese bearing long poles, at the top of which there was a painted cube or sphere, from which strips of paper were hanging. These devices were to represent the fire-god, whose presence is expected to put out the fire; or, that failing, to prevent its extending.

The crowd was a docile one and was easily kept outside of the line. When I had spent some time watching the China-men bringing their effects out of the burning building, and was wondering how they had managed to stow away so much trash in so small a place, they were still at it. Finally, when the house was destroyed there came a party with long bamboo ladders, which they rested against the next building, and, without any apparent reason, for the danger was over, they clambered up and down like so many monkeys. Fires usually do great damage in such towns as this, and thus the excitement is easily accounted for. I would have been sorry to miss seeing the crowd, which was interesting because of the varied elements of which it was composed.

I have been at Tokio three times, have visited several Buddhist temples, have seen no end of Japanese curios, beautiful pottery, fine lacquered ware, superb bronzes and delicate carvings. Although I shall never become learned in those things, the terms Satsuma, Kaga, Owari, Hizen, etc., have more of a meaning for me than ever before. The curio shops of Yokohama are better worth visiting than those of Tokio.

The natural beauties of this country (and I am told there are greater in store for me than any I have yet seen) cannot, it seems to me, be too highly praised. The finest flowers here (this is the home of the Chrysanthemum and the *Camellia Japonica*) are odorless.

VIII. A Japanese Restaurant.

Yokohama, May 25, 1887.

I arose at a late hour this morning, having had a somewhat uncomfortable night. Nothing more than a cold shiver now and then, that caused me to fear that I had a touch of malaria. Having kept well thus far, I had no notion of succumbing to the climate, and so began the day with a dose of quinine. When I got down stairs it was half past eight o'clock. At eleven o'clock, I took the train for Tokio, where I had an appointment with Mr. Ngato Shiraishi, Professor of Engineering at the Imperial College of Japan, and also with Mr. R. Masujima, President of the Law School and one of the leading lawyers of Japan.

The railway ride to Tokio was not the

less interesting because of its being the fourth time I made the trip. The names of Kanagawa, Tsurumi, Omori, and the other stations have already quite a familiar sound, although, much as it is with us at home, I would defy anyone to recognize them as pronounced by the railway officials. On the train I met Mr. Robertson, of Van Tine & Co., the New York importers of Chinese and Japanese goods, and Dr. Eldridge, of Yokohama. Mr. Robertson, having learned from my good friend H. M. Roberts, Esq., of Yokohama, that I intend to visit China, gave me some useful information and advice anent travelling in that country. Dr. Eldridge has been in Japan about seventeen years, having at first been in the employ of the Government. He is now practising medicine at Yokohama, and also delivers lectures on Medical Jurisprudence at the Tokio Law School. When I spoke to him of the politeness of the Japanese, he remarked that it is much less elaborate than in former years, and added that, with many of the people, the old-time Japanese politeness has disappeared, while nothing has been adopted as a substitute for it. It was not an infrequent occurrence, during the earlier years of his residence in this country, to see two *daimios*, meeting on the road, alight from their horses and spend quite a while in the bowing and scraping that the rigid etiquette of the olden time prescribed. Having gone through the proper motions, they would again mount their steeds, and each would go his way.

I mentioned the playing of the band of the *Brooklyn* yesterday, and told the Doctor how much I had enjoyed hearing the strains of "Marching through Georgia," although any other American air would have served equally well. Whereupon, reviewing olden memories of his own, he told me how, on the first or second night after his arrival at Tokio, he was sitting, lonely and just a little homesick, in his room, afraid to venture out of doors without a guard, for in those days the feeling against the foreigner was strong, and two-sworded bravos would waylay him if he came their way. When he was in the depths of the "blues" he heard steps on the veranda, and some one near by whistling "Marching through Georgia." A moment later, a young Japanese entered and, introducing himself, said, "I am ——, and have been assigned as your secretary and interpreter."

After exchanging greetings, the Doctor's first words were: "I heard some one whistling, a moment ago. Can you tell me who it was?"

The young man stammered an apology, saying, "It was I; I didn't know you were so near by. Please excuse me."

"Don't apologize," answered the Doctor. "I am really much obliged to you."

While I am in the story-telling mood, I will give you a good *mot* that I heard a few evenings since. While dining with us, a guest to whom a glass of wine was offered thus excused himself for declining to accept it:

"Many years ago, when I was quite a young man, I was an attaché of our legation at ———. My chief employment was to wait upon the Minister every morning and consult with him upon the *ménu* for the dinner of that day. My judgment of wines was, for one so young as I, quite a good one, and I had a fine field for its exercise. Well, to make a short story of a long one, the Minister is dead, and I have the gout. So, please excuse me."

I lunched at the Tokio Club, where, at about 2 P. M., Mr. Shiraishi called for me. We visited the Technological Department of the Tokio College (or University, I forget which), where I was shown through several of the rooms. I was especially pleased with the large and well-lighted library, containing about 20,000 volumes, and the laboratory.

After that, as I had expressed a wish to

see some Japanese acrobats, we took *jin-ricshas* and started for a place where an exhibition of wrestling was to be given. It was at quite a distance from the College. On our way we passed by the walls and moat that surround the former palace of the Tycoon, saw the barracks of the Imperial Guard, the parade ground where squads of soldiers were going through a drill in gymnastics, and, travelling through a section of Tokio that was new to me, I was again impressed by the great size of the city. Finally, we reached the place where the show was to be given, only to find it closed.

Thereupon, Mr. S. suggested that we visit a Japanese restaurant, one not frequented by Europeans, but in which the customs of the country are observed. It was one of the best class. On entering, we were met by a number of attendants, male and female, who knelt on the ground and in token of welcome bent their bodies until their foreheads touched the floor.

Every portion of the house was scrupu-
lously clean, and, to prevent its being
soiled with the dirt of the street, all who
enter are expected to take off their shoes
at the threshold and either walk about in
their stocking feet or wear the straw sandals that are provided for their use. We
did as we were bid to do, and were then
shown into a room on the second floor.
There were no chairs; but pretty cushions
were brought, that we might squat upon
them. The floor was of straw matting;
not carpet-wise as we use it, but in slabs
about two inches in thickness and, say,
three feet by six in size. The one side of
the room was of sash work, with panes of
glass running across the centre, while the
top and bottom were "glazed" with paper.
The girl who waited on us was prettily
dressed; her hair was elaborately arranged
and was quite glossy with the cocoanut
oil that had been used in dressing it; her
feet were bare.

She brought us various dishes and

some *sakc*, or millet wine. It tastes much like dry sherry, and is served warm. I wrestled with the chopsticks and essayed some of the dishes. Then we sent for *gaishas* (singing and dancing girls). Two came. The dancing was stupid and the singing doleful. The singer accompanied herself on the *samisen* and sang in such style that I could not see what need there was for her being so particular about tuning her instrument.

As it was getting late in the afternoon, I left in order to attend a dinner of the faculty of the Law School, to which Mr. Masujima had kindly invited me. Mr. M. was one of the projectors of the institution, which, although started only a few years ago, already has some 1,200 or 1,300 students and a faculty of about twenty-five professors. Among the invited guests were Consul Greathouse and Mr. Sidmore, his assistant; Mr. Litchfield, an English barrister residing at Yokohama, and Mr. George T. Bromley, late U. S. Consul at

Tientsin. Excepting myself, the rest of the company consisted of Japanese lawyers and judges. The evening was a very pleasant one. There were some excellent speeches and a cordial interchange of congratulations on the undoubted success of the Law School. The party broke up at about 9 P.M., and, taking the 9.45 P.M. train, I returned to Yokohama.

IX. Some Japanese Customs.

Yokohama, May 26th, 1887.

There are various odd features (that is, they seem odd to a stranger) that are worth noting. For instance, I do not think it would pay to import hods into this country, for this is the way they get around the need of them: A man standing on the sidewalk makes a round ball of a lump of mortar and throws it to another man on the scaffolding, who passes it on in the same way until it reaches its destination.

You can see tailors sitting in their shops and holding the piece of goods on which they are working between the great toe and the next, and I have seen wood-carvers holding the pieces they were carving in the same way.

Then, too, you ought to see the women with blackened teeth and shaved eyebrows. These are married women, and are expected thus to disfigure themselves lest they may prove too attractive to men to whom they are not married. I am told that the custom does not obtain so generally as in former years, but I see many examples of this sort of disfigurement whenever I visit the Japanese quarter of Yokohama or Homura. It is even asserted that old maids, envious of the distinction of the matrons, also blacken their teeth and shave their eyebrows. Many of the married women who do this are quite young. I cannot doubt that the desired result is thus achieved, although I should think that it might have another and unlooked-for effect, viz: in putting their own husbands out of conceit of them.

As to the *jin-ricsha* coolies, I found it well to acquaint myself with the regular tariff fixed for their services. If you hand one of them the exact amount to which he is entitled, he accepts it grate-fully. If you give him more, he presumes on a foreigner's ignorance and insists that he is underpaid. It is only when you have come to know your man that you can safely indulge your good nature by giving him, in addition to his fee, a *pourboire*. That the *jin-ricsha* coolies deserve better pay than they usually get for their work is beyond ques-tion. The Japanese, however, manage to get more for their money than we foreigners do, for I have often seen husband, wife and child crowded into one *jin-ricsha*.

It seems to me that the hardest worked among the natives are the coolies who push and pull the carts that serve the same purpose as carts or drays do with us. As horses and mules are scarce here, and human labor cheap, this work is done by men. Five or six of them will toil along the highway, struggling with their

heavy load, and gasping, rather than singing, a monotonous sort of chant. No one
of them sings more than two or three
notes; as soon as he stops another takes
it up, and thus it goes on unceasingly.

In the warm season these folks are not
burdened with overmuch clothing. In
this respect there is, I am told, even
greater freedom in those sections to
which the foreigner has not yet been
admitted. In the open ports, Japanese
police regulations insist on a certain
measure of deference to European notions
on this point. In Yokohama, if report
speaks truly, there are bathing establishments where the sexes bathe together
indiscriminately.

As an illustration of native ignorance
and innocence, I will repeat what an
English gentleman, who has lived here
during many years, told me the other
day. In the course of business, he once
called on a reputable and well-to-do
Japanese tradesman. He was a frequent

visitor, and had become very fond of the baby of the household, rarely omitting to bring some sweetmeat or trinket for the youngster. On this occasion, he pushed back the unbarred gate and, in walking towards the house, was obliged to pass Madam, who was comfortably bathing in a tub. He politely ignored her, and she seemed to take no notice of his presence. He stopped for a moment to fondle the little fellow, who was playing in the yard, and offered him a toy that he had brought for him. The child was shy, and drew back as if afraid. Quick as thought, the mother stepped from her bath, took the toy from his hands, gave it to the child, bowed politely, and uttering the word *arigato* (thanks) returned to her tub.

*   *   *   *   *   *   *   *

As there has been no outgoing steamer since I wrote you about the Shiba temples, I will add a brief account of the Asakusa Temple, which is also in Tokio, but quite remote from the former.

Shiba is silent, solemn, dreary; Asakusa full of life. It was on a Sunday that B. and I visited it, but I am told that crowds as great as we saw can be found there every day in the year. It is approached through a long narrow avenue, lined on either side with shops and booths, in which are displayed all sorts of wares, such as one would find in the *Ginza*, but with a noticeable preponderance of sweetmeats, toys, little books with bright colored covers, fans, ornaments for the hair, and paper umbrellas. Then, too, there are voluble medicine men, selling lotions and potent draughts, on the merits of which they are expatiating to the gaping crowd about them. Besides these, there are old women with jars of the world-famed, pretty three-tailed goldfish of Japan, and others offering for sale birds of all sorts. Indeed, the approach to Asakusa Temple suggests a combination of a country fair and the pink lemonade and peanut environment of an American travelling circus show.

The temple is full of people, mostly women and children, with a sprinkling of old men. There are priests and acolytes at the altar. Women kneel at a sort of grating, and before leaving drop a coin between the bars. All is noise and bustle. Flocks of tame pigeons have made their nests up among the rafters and fly hither and thither as if used to the crowds about them. The decorations, although more profuse than at Shiba, are, as a rule, of a cheaper and more popular sort. We are especially interested by the large grotesque paintings of saints and warriors, and by the huge paper lanterns suspended from the beams in the roof. Then, too, there are several large bronze vases of unmistakable antiquity and beautiful workmanship.

It was well worth our while to visit Asakusa, for the sake of noting the contrast between it and Shiba. I shall,

however, spare you any further description of Japanese temples, now that I
have written about these two, for I am
informed that when you have seen one
you have seen all. Still, judging from
the pictures and the accounts I have
received, those at Nikko surpass all others
in beauty and in size. I fear, however,
that I shall not find time to visit that
section of Japan, although I have had
most tempting invitations to do so.

X. THE BLUFF AT YOKOHAMA.

Grand Hotel,
Yokohama, May 28, 1887.

* * * * The Grand Hotel is, of
course, in the foreign quarter, which is
largely given up to business concerns and
the commodious establishments of the
foreign consuls. I have been a frequent
visitor at the American Consulate, and
am indebted to Consul Greathouse and
Mr. Sidmore, his assistant, for various
kind attentions. I find the Consul eager
to forward the interests of Americans in
Japan, and can bear testimony to his
efforts in that direction. If those among
our manufacturers who wish to trade
with the Japanese would go to the
trouble of studying the market, so as
to acquire a knowledge of just what

kinds of goods are wanted here, they would find it greatly to their advantage. Instead of doing this, they have often experimented by sending out articles for which they could find no buyers at home. Encountering the rivalry of the keen-witted and careful competitors who have the advantage of being on the spot, such experiments, as might well be expected, have generally resulted in financial loss and discouragement.

I have passed many pleasant hours with various members of the German colony which forms quite an important section of the foreign population of Yokohama. They are all actively engaged in business, some as chiefs in charge of agencies, others in subordinate yet important positions. They are active, bright men, and are rated as among the cleverest merchants hereabouts. My letter to Mr. D., at whose pleasant home I **was** most cordially welcomed, **was** the means of my meeting these people, who, far away from their Fatherland, have nevertheless managed to preserve much of their German *Gemüthlichkeit*. I consider myself fortunate in having made their acquaintance, and sometimes wonder whether, after leaving here, I shall ever again chance across any of these pleasant companions.

A creek, or canal, emptying into the Bay at the right of the Grand Hotel, separates Yokohama proper from the Bluff, which is the residence quarter of most of the Americans and Europeans who dwell here. There are pretty cottages, or rather bungalows, vine-covered and almost hidden by the trees and bushes. While the greater number are of modest proportions, there are some of more pretentious appearance. Nearly all of them have an air of comfort and refinement, and, so far as I have been favored with an opportunity to inform myself on the subject, I have found that the interiors made good the impression suggested by the outside view. Many of them are surrounded by carefully kept grounds in which Japanese gardeners have had their own sweet will, as is readily seen from the abundance of dwarf maples of varied colorings, and the stunted and distorted pines and cedars. Then, too, there are the miniature bridges, spanning tiny rivulets, under overhanging willows, such as the devices on Japanese pottery have long since made known to us. To complete the picture, the little lady in the costume of the country, with umbrella in one hand and fan in the other, and with eyes looking northwest and northeast at the same time, ought to be on the bridge.

The Stars and Stripes are flying from the flag-staff of the U. S. Naval Hospital, the first building to the right as you ascend the hillside. It is in charge of Dr. D. McMurtrie, U. S. N., whose cosy dwelling is hard by and within the same compound. The Doctor has been stationed here for some time, and both he and Mrs. M. are deservedly great favorites in Yokohama.

Leaving the Hospital and continuing along the Bluff, you travel up hill and down dale, through lanes of cottages such as I have mentioned, and, after getting beyond the dwellings, you reach the race-course, where, a few days ago, I attended one of the meetings. The runners were of the native breed of ponies, the riders were Japanese *bettos* (grooms). The races are an event of some importance hereabouts. On the days of the meetings, the foreign business houses and banks close at noon, and it is well worth one's while to attend for the sake of seeing assembled nearly all there is of foreign society at Yokohama.

On our way back to the hotel, we made somewhat of a detour, taking the drive along Mississippi Bay and through the fishing village (I cannot recall its name) that lies seaward beyond the Bluff. The scene, as we drove along the shore, was

one of rare beauty. The day was drawing
to a close. The clouds varied in color
from a rosy purple to a delicate violet and
the brighter tints were reflected and soft-
ened in the waters of the Bay, whose surface was as smooth as a mill-pond. It
was one of those happy moments that
make the young and the romantic wish
that it might continue thus forever.

Seated in the same carriage with me
were a youth and a maiden who probably
felt just that way, while I was thinking
about dinner. I had been watching their
romance for some days. A few evenings later, I met them again at a dinner
somewhere on the Bluff. There was a
fine moon that night, for their special
benefit I imagine, and when the party
broke up they said that they would rather
walk home than ride. Well, they had their
walk and, I suppose, their talk; for since
then I have had the pleasure of congratu-
lating them on their betrothal.

Directly across the Canal, on the lowland to the right of the Bluff, is the village of **Homura**, a sort of suburb of Yokohama. It is thickly settled, the streets are narrow, the houses closely huddled together, and, while there are shops and artificers of various kinds, the chief product, at first blush, appears to consist of Japanese babies. There are so many of them that it is sometimes difficult to get out of their way. B. amuses himself by giving them small copper coins and is soon the centre of an admiring crowd. There are babies of all sizes, the large ones carrying the smaller, toddlers of six or seven years with their infant brothers or sisters. strapped to their backs—a settlement of live Japanese dolls, as it were.

I must not forget to mention **Fujita**, or the House of the Hundred Steps. The most direct way of getting there is to use the steep stone stairs, of just one hundred steps, that lead from the **end** of one of the streets of **Homura** up to the top of the Bluff. There is an easier but longer approach from the other side.

It is visited for the sake of the fine sunsets, for the extended view of Yokohama and the Bay, and, when the skies are clear, of distant Fujiama. The place belongs to the Tanabe family, and is in charge of the two clever Misses Tanabe who, with their brother, Tanabe Gengoro, are interested in a successful silk shop in Homura. The Hundred Steps House is much affected by most foreigners who visit Yokohama. If you choose, you can have a cup of tea, a glass of wine, or other simple refreshment. You are politely served by the female attendants, one of whom, for some inscrutable reason, has been nicknamed "Jimmy." As the Tanabes and Jimmy are bright, clever women, with pleasant manners, who are able to converse in English, French, German or Russian, it is easy to understand how their establishment has come to be a favorite lounging place. After a visitor has enjoyed the views again and again, he will still find it worth his while to climb the hundred steps for the sake of lounging away an hour or two at Fujita. A seat overlooking the hillside; a companion ready for a chat when you are in the mood, but not conversational enough to force you to talk against your will; and that other good comrade, a cigar: with these elements you will find it pleasant enough to end up the day there, doing a little quiet lotus-eating on your own account, and intérrupted only by Jimmy's "Donzhu want some more tea?" or the antics of mischievous Cheesi (a diminutive relative of the Tanabes), whose great delight it is to tease the visitors.

XI. TREATY REVISION, ETC.

In certain circles the closely related topics of extra-territoriality and treaty-revision are frequently canvassed. Both Japanese and foreigners find much to object to under existing conditions; but, while both sides ask for added privileges, they do not find it so easy to concede what is wanted of them. Perhaps this is hardly just to the position of the Japanese, for they are only asking back what, because of their weakness, they surrendered to the great powers. At present legal causes in which foreigners are interested are conducted before the consular courts, and, as a consequence, there are as many different jurisdictions as there are nationalities represented here. The Japanese object to this, feeling that such a position of affairs is inconsistent with the dignity of a sovereign and independent nation. **The** government, knowing that the treaties stand in the way of the change so greatly desired by it, has within the last few years invited the assistance of foreign jurisconsults in the preparation of new civil, commercial and criminal codes, in the hope that it will be practicable to procure the consent of the treaty powers to the proposed change. As an inducement to the foreign governments to permit their citizens to have their causes tried before Japanese courts and by the laws of the land, the government is willing to have those powers appoint judges who are to sit with the native judges in the trial of causes affecting the rights of foreigners. Another important feature is that, with the acceptance of this condition, all parts of the empire will be opened to foreigners, who, at present, are restricted to trading or owning property in the few free ports.

On the part of the government, the
revision or abrogation of the treaties is
desired for another important reason; for
it would permit of a change in the import
duties. The present tariff is merely a
nominal one, which, while it yields a
certain amount of revenue, was framed
solely in the interest of the foreign high
contracting powers.

Thus far all attempts at revision have
proved abortive. The foreigners, as a
rule, are satisfied with the present condition of affairs, or, at best, want no
change unless it be in the direction of
added privileges for themselves. Their
interests are purely commercial; not
national. That patriotic Japanese must
find much to chafe at in this state
of affairs follows as a matter of course.
In the meanwhile, with unmistakable
patience and apparent good nature, they
bide their time.

XII. A Japanese Dinner.

Yokohama, May 29, 1887.

It has been raining incessantly since yesterday noon, and just now it is pouring at a rate that must be very discouraging to pleasure seekers and livery-stable keepers.

In spite of the rain, I went to Tokio last evening, to attend a dinner given by Mr. Masujima. At the banquet to the faculty of the Law School, and at which I was his guest, the service was in the European style. On this occasion, it was his desire that the foreigners in the party should see how the Japanese live among themselves. He had invited about twenty-four gentlemen, one-third of whom were Americans or Europeans, and the remaining two-thirds Japanese. The latter were, all of them, attired in the costume of the country.

After leaving the Shinbashi Station at Tokio I rode for about half an hour in a *jin-ricsha*. For the greater part of the way our route lay through a quarter of the city that was quite new to me and finer than any portion of Tokio I had yet seen. I was told afterward that it is the most aristocratic section of the city. When I reached the restaurant, a sort of private club-house, where we were to be entertained, I found that it was on a hill overlooking a beautiful little valley and surrounded with fine trees and shrubbery. The place and its surroundings were so picturesque that I could only wish for a chance to see it all in fine weather. On our way thither I got the impression that we were going into a section devoted to semi-detached suburban villas, such as we have on the outskirts of our cities. Looking through the trees, I could, how-ever, distinguish closely-built streets in various directions, and was told that we were, so to say, in the heart of Tokio.

On entering, we removed our shoes, as is the custom of the country; the proper sequel to this would have been to follow the example of our Japanese friends and put on the straw sandals that were provided for us. Unfortunately, however, our socks were not made with thumbs, and, as a result, we were obliged to remain in our stocking feet for the rest of the evening. One of our party had the forethought to provide himself with felt slippers. The floor was, as usual, covered with slabs of straw matting, and the rooms, although larger, were in nearly all respects much like that in the restaurant I visited in company with Mr. Shiraishi some days ago.

There were no chairs, and I found sitting on my haunches rather fatiguing. I therefore changed my position from time to time, but did not attempt to sit on my feet, as the lithe and slender Japanese are wont to do. To one with my figure, and without previous practice, that would have been an impossibility. Indeed, my back still aches from the efforts I made to balance myself while enjoying the dinner.

We were first invited to the upper floor of the building, where we took part in a ceremonious tea drinking. One of the Japanese gentlemen, assisted by others, went through certain forms, according to an old-time ritual prescribed for such occasions. When every guest had partaken of a cup of the delicious tea that had been thus prepared, we were invited to descend to the ground floor, where the dinner was to be served.

The guests were ranged along the sides of the large room, and the viands were brought to each one on a lacquered tray, by pretty Japanese girls. Each course was served in a lacquered cup with cover; when you had tasted of it, you replaced the cover and left the cup standing before you. By the time the dinner was over there were some dozen or more of the cups in front of each guest. We drank *sake*, which was served warm and in tiny porcelain cups. They gave us soup, rice, boiled tay (the favorite fish of Japan, and excellent), salmon trout, sea-weed, etc., etc.; some of them savory and palatable; others, to one unaccustomed to them, impossible. For the soups, we were provided with porcelain spoons; knives and forks were not to be seen, for this was a chopstick affair.

For the entertainment of the guests, there was a performance of sleight-of-hand tricks, some of which were marvellously well done, the cleverest performer in the troupe being an urchin apparently not over twelve years old. There were, also, Japanese songs, singing and dancing by Japanese girls, besides songs and humorous speeches by some of the foreign guests. How long the festivities were kept up I am unable to say, as those of us who wanted to take the last train for Yokohama were obliged to leave at about ten o'clock. Those whom we left there seemed to think that very early, hardly "the shank of the evening" as John Phenix has it.

It was a most interesting entertainment, affording me a glimpse of Japanese ways that I might not have found it easy to obtain otherwise. For this and other courtesies I have abundant reason to be grateful for the constant kindness of Mr. Masujima.

XIII. KOBÉ–NAGASAKI.

On board the S. S. Satsuma-Maru,
          Nagasaki, June 4, 1887.

We left Yokohama on the 31st of
May, at noon, in the S. S. *Satsuma-
Maru*, Captain Conner commanding. The
steamer is, I understand, the smallest in
the fleet, and is owned by the Jananese
company known as the *Nippon Yusen
Kaisha*. This organization controls a
fleet of one hundred or more steam
vessels. A few of the older ones formerly
belonged to the Pacific Mail S. S. Company; the larger portion were built on
the Clyde.

At seven P.M. of Wednesday, June 1st,
we reached Kobé, where we remained until six P.M. of the following day. Since
leaving Kobé we have made two stops;

at Shimonosaki, where we remained about an hour or more, and at Nagasski, where we dropped anchor at six o'clock A.M. (about an hour ago). We shall leave here this evening or sometime to-morrow, sailing across the China Sea, direct for Shanghai, which point we hope to reach late on Monday or early on Tuesday next.

Among our passengers was an intelligent and agreeable Scotchman who came to Yokohama some eighteen years ago, at the call of the Japanese government, and who was in its employ some eight years, superintending the erection of light-houses. He knows the coast thoroughly, and had much that was interesting to tell us about various points we passed, as well as about Japan and the Japanese. I was very sorry to part company with him when we reached here, for this is his journey's end.

Writing from Yokohama the other day, I expressed my regret at not having touched a fiddle since I left the States, and added that I would manage to beg, borrow or steal one as soon as I reached Shanghai. It occurred to me, after I had posted my letter, that it would be just as proper to buy one, but that, although the more creditable method, was really an afterthought.

It was so late in the day when we reached Kobé that I concluded I would dine on the steamer before going ashore. That same evening I called on Mr. B., whom a friend in Yokohama had apprised of my intended visit. I had been there but a little while when I found that Mrs. B. is an accomplished pianist and, as our steamer was not to leave until the next evening, I gladly accepted her invitation for an hour or two of sonata practising on the following afternoon. One of the two violins in the settlement was borrowed for the occasion and, for the first time since I left home, I had the pleasure of hugging a violin. In my wildest dreams it had never occurred to me that I would one day be playing a Beethoven sonata in Japan.

Kobé is, to my notion, a far prettier town than Yokohama. This is the name of the foreign settlement adjoining Hiogo; the latter designation is found on most of the maps, while Kobé is marked on but few of them. The foreign settlement at Kobé is neither so old nor so extensive as that at Yokohama. On the other hand, the buildings, as a rule, are finer, and the streets wider and cleaner. The beautiful green hills back of the town form a fine background to the picture. Some of the foreign residents have made their homes in bungalows two or three hundred feet above the foot of the hills, and from one of these (the residence of Captain D. J. Carroll), where I took luncheon, the view of the town, the shipping in the harbor, and the sea and islands for miles beyond, was very fine. Captain Carroll was, I am informed, the first white man to settle here, and has been one of the prominent European residents of Japan since a date immediately following the arrival of Commodore Perry.

The forenoon of the day I spent at Kobé was passed in visiting curio shops and the spacious and comfortable building of the Kobé Club. After leaving Kobé we entered the famous Inland Sea, or rather strait, between the islands Nippon and Kinsiu. I wish I could describe the matchless beauty of the Inland Sea. For hours our course lay among and between islands seemingly without number, and of all sizes and shapes. They are all verdure clad. Some are not more than a few feet in diameter, others are large enough to furnish homes for settlements of the fishermen whose myriad boats, meeting the eye at every turn, add greatly to the charm of the scene.

Nagasaki, June 6, 1887.

I propose to send you a letter on Japanese writing paper; that is, if I can manage to keep my pen from going through it. This is of the quality generally used by the natives, except that, because of the pictures, it is especially elegant. The Japanese write with a hair pencil steeped in India ink, and thus the flimsy texture of the paper does not bother them as it now does me.

We arrived here yesterday at daylight, and the intention was to leave at five o'clock in the afternoon. It stormed so severely all day that the Captain thought it would be wiser not to venture outside, and so our departure was delayed until this afternoon at four o'clock. If all goes well, we shall reach Shanghai in a little less than two days.

Nagasaki is the great coaling station of Japan, the most important mines in the Empire being near by. The Japanese town is quite extensive; the foreign settlement is small, although the amount of business transacted here is said to be large.

Great quantities of rice are shipped from here, and the fine harbor affords ample room for a large amount of shipping. French, German, English and Japanese merchant steamers are now lying at anchor here, and one large Russian frigate is on the dry dock, which is said to be the largest this side of Suez.

It would amuse you to see how they load vessels with coal. The barges or lighters are rowed up alongside of the vessel that is to receive the coal. Men are down in the hold busily filling the baskets, which are handed along from one helper to the other, until they reach the vessel. These helpers form a line, and do not stand more than two feet apart. Most of this work is done by girls, and when, as with the collier lying near by, you can see about six or seven hundred of them at it at one and the same

time, it is a busy scene. Although each
worker remains in the one place until
the task is completed, the movement
of arms and baskets makes it look as if
the great crowd was trying to climb up
the ship's side.

Yesterday being very stormy, we had
what is known as regular Nagasaki
weather. Indeed, the sailors jokingly
tell us that it rains here about eight days
out of the seven. We have had "leaky"
weather ever since our arrival. Notwithstanding the rain, I went ashore yesterday
in a *sampan*, and visited the shops of some
of the workers in tortoise shell, a branch of
industry for which Nagasaki has quite a
reputation. After an hour thus spent, I
was glad to return to the steamer and to
remain there for the rest of the day.

This morning the weather promised to
mend, and I went ashore again, looked in
at some porcelain and curio shops, and
visited two bazars, making a few purchases in several of them.

The harbor of Nagasaki is almost land-locked, the town lying at the foot and along the sides of the green hills that encircle it like an amphitheatre. It looks prettier and more inviting from the ship than it proves on shore. It has all the usual features of a busy maritime town. Jack-tars of various nationalities abound, and in the foreign quarter there is quite a number of queer looking taverns that seem to have been intended for the special entertainment of sailors.

There are five Russian men-of-war lying in the harbor. This morning we heard the band on the Admiral's ship playing the Russian national anthem, and it was well played, too.

As most of the people I meet imagine that I am travelling for pleasure, I am often told that I ought to have visited China before going to Japan, and thus have left the best for the last. From their point of view they are probably in the right, and I do not feel called upon to tell them just why I am here. My stay in this country began on the 15th of May and to-day I leave it. I have spent three delightful weeks in Japan, during which I have seen much that is worth remembering, although both tourists and old residents assure me that to have missed Nikko and Kioto is not to have seen Japan at all.

Perhaps I shall find time on my return to visit those points. If not, I shall be duly grateful for all that I have seen. For the present, however, I must bid farewell to *Dai Nippon.*

XIV. SHANGHAI.

Astor House,
Shanghai, June 9, 1887.

We left Nagasaki at about 5 P.M. on
Sunday, the 5th inst., in a drizzling rain.
When we awoke on Monday the sky was
clear and bright, and our staunch little
steamer was carrying us due West on the
blue waters of the Yellow Sea. We
were out of sight of land during the
whole of that day. On Tuesday morning, the 7th, we were no longer in blue
water, but were sailing through what in
color resembled pea soup. The discolora-
tion of the sea is caused by the great
quantity of silt carried to the ocean by
the Yang-tse-Kiang River and is noticeable at a distance of about sixty miles from
the Coast. The great stream is very wide at

its mouth and the banks are so low that one is hardly apt to notice having entered it. At about noon we dropped anchor at Wusung, a shipping town at the mouth of the Whangpoa River, a tributary of the Yang-tse-Kiang. We lay there an hour or two, waiting for high tide, and then steamed up the Whangpoa to Shanghai, which is about sixteen miles from Wusung.

We arrived here at about four o'clock on the afternoon of the 7th, and proceeded at once to the Astor House, where we have comfortable quarters. This is the principal American hotel in Shanghai; Mr. Janssen, the landlord, is from Newburgh, N. Y. Near by is the American Consulate; beyond that, the offices and wharves of the Japanese S. S. Company. Nearly opposite my room is the fine building of the German Consulate.

I have thus far not seen enough of Shanghai to say much about it. I have been kept too busy to find much time for

sight-seeing. What I have seen, however, has impressed me very favorably.
Shanghai is the most important shipping
point in China. While the Japanese
Company (the *Nippon Yusen Kaisha*)
keeps up a weekly service between this
point and Yokohama, calling by the way
at Nagasaki and Kobé, there are constant arrivals of colliers and junks from
Nagasaki and other ports in Japan.
Steamers of the North German Lloyd, of
the *Messageries Maritimes*, and of the P.
and O. Company, carry mails and passengers to Europe, *via* Hong Kong or Singa-
pore. Besides these, there are ocean
tramps sailing to European and American ports, with cargoes of tea or silk.
The China Merchant Steam Navigation
Company, the great firm of Jardine, Mattheson & Co., and also that of Butterfield
& Swire, control quite a fleet of steamers
that ply between this city, the commercial capital of the empire, and the coast
and river towns. Add to these a goodly

number of sailing vessels of foreign
build, countless junks of all sizes, some
Chinese men-of-war, an English frigate or
two, a German ditto, a couple of opium
hulks, and a host of *sampans* rushing
hither and thither, and you can readily
understand that there is much to be seen
at the Shanghai water-side.

As I have not been outside of the
foreign settlement, and have in fact been
in only two or three of its streets, the
sights I have seen can hardly be called
Chinese. There are many large buildings
in the way of banks, warehouses, consular
offices, hotels and private residences.
Although the foreign population is said
to be only 5,000, the buildings used by it
cover so large a space, the streets are so
wide and so full of life, and the shipping,
as I have already mentioned, so numerous,
that Shanghai easily gives one the impression of a large city. In my case, this
may, in a measure, be owing to my having just come from Japan, where nearly

all the houses are low and the streets, as a rule, narrow.

As a gathering place for all sorts of nationalities, Shanghai is even more important than Yokohama. Besides Europeans and Americans, you meet Sikhs, Singhalese, Parsees, Japanese, etc. The Sikhs are the police of the English settlement. They are tall, very dark, and have piercing black eyes. Up to yesterday, they wore a dark-blue uniform; to-day they are in summer costume of white jean, and with their swarthy faces, black beards and crimson turbans, they present quite a picturesque appearance. They do not understand the Chinese language, nor do the natives understand theirs. I am told, however, that this trifling circumstance does not interfere with the successful performance of their duty as preservers of the peace.

The *jin-ricsha* is to be found here as well as in Japan, where it was invented. Then, too, there is the Chinese barrow,

with a wheel through the middle—a sort
of centre-board wheel-barrow—which is
used only by the Chinese. You will see
one, two, or three passengers sitting on
either side, their feet dangling in the air.
On a photograph that I have just bought,
there is a Chinaman being wheeled home
from market. He is on one side of the
vehicle, and a pig is strapped to the other.
The barrow is, I understand, even cheaper
as a means of conveyance than the *jin-
ricsha*, for the use of which the charge is
ten cents per hour.

The foreign settlement is divided into
the American, the British and the French
concessions, and of these the British is
by far the largest and most important.
Coming up the stream, the American
concession is first reached. The principal
business street in this section is named
Broadway, and is largely given up to
Chinese shop-keepers. There are, I am
informed, about 150,000 natives who, for
business and other reasons, have found it

worth their while to live in the Settlement
and outside of the walls of the old town.
They prefer being under the jurisdiction
of the Municipal Council to subjecting
themselves to the capricious and at times
exacting "squeezes" of the native officials
of Shanghai proper. Some of them have
fine shops in the best quarters and are
regarded as honorable merchants; that
they are very shrewd at driving a bar-
gain, I am, from my own experience,
quite willing to believe.

The American quarter is known as
Hongkew. In this are situated the Astor
House, the American Consulate, the German Consulate, the offices and wharves
of the Japanese Steamer Company, the
docks and ship-yards of Farnham & Co.,
and factories of various kinds.

Crossing the Soochow Creek by a little
bridge, you enter the British settlement.
To the left is the pretty Public Garden,
and at this point the Bund begins. It
extends into the French quarter, where it

is known as *Quai de France*. The line of
demarcation between John Bull's domain
and that of Jean Crapaud is a lazy, black
looking and ill-smelling stream known as
Yang King Pang Creek. To-day we
shall not cross it, but will remain in the
English settlement. The Bund is a fine,
wide highway, with trees on either side.
Just beyond the end of the Garden
bridge, and to the right of the Public
Garden, are the buildings and the fine
grounds of the British Consulate. Among
other noteworthy edifices are the Masonic
Hall, the offices of Jardine, Mattheson &
Co., the Hong Kong and Shanghai Bank,
and the large building of Russell & Co.,
the leading American house in this
quarter of the globe. The firm of
Sassoon, Sons & Co. have commodious
and pleasant quarters that stand back
some distance from the street and are
approached through a long, shaded
avenue, that suggests the entrance to a
private residence rather than to a business

house.   Large undertakings, requiring considerable sums of money to support them and a long time for their development, are entered into by the more important firms hereabouts, but everything seems to be done in a leisurely way. No one is ever in a hurry, unless it be on steamer day, when principals and clerks will often work all night in order to bring their correspondence up to the day, and almost the very hour, of sailing. If there be hard work, that is left to the coolies. A *comprador* or a *shroff* is never in a hurry, but, in the words of the song, he "gets there, all the same."

Enter a bank and ask for a draft on Yokohama, Tashkend or any point you may think of, for these people have trade and money connections all over the world. After you have told the polite clerk the amount you wish to remit, he calls the *shroff*, who is at once silver expert and paymaster, and asks him to make the calculation, which is speedily done on the *saroban*, or abacus, which throughout China and Japan is used for this purpose. When the clerk gets his answer, he may look up at the clock and then ask you to return at, say, 2 P. M. for your draft. You wonder why the transaction cannot be completed at once, and when you meekly express your thoughts on the subject, you are gently, but firmly, told that it is so near tiffin time that it would be impossible to accommodate you until the hour named. It seems so much a matter of course that you have not a word to say. You have simply made acquaintance with another custom of the country, and are sensible enough to be glad of that fact.

Since he mentions it, you remember that you have promised to take tiffin with some friends at the Shanghai Club, and, availing yourself of the services of the ever-ready *jin-ricsha*, you go to the club-house. In the wine room you will find a large representation of the business world of Shanghai, who meet there daily at high noon, as at a sort of exchange. For comfort and completeness, the quarters of the Shanghai Club would do credit to any club in any city. In its large rooms the swinging *punkah* causes you to forget the torrid heat of the streets, and its excellent library and well-furnished newspaper room have helped me to while away many an otherwise tedious hour.

But I quite forget that you went to the club for tiffin. The meal was served in the large dining-room upstairs and, with the charming company assembled to discuss it, you could not but enjoy the meeting. As it happened, you did not get back to the bank until long after two o'clock; and when you did reach it you learned about another custom of the bankers hereabouts. They will wait on you after three o'clock as cheerfully as before that hour, and rarely get away until four. I suppose this is their way of averaging up the tiffin account.

XV. STREET SCENES, ETC.

The streets in the English settlement are named after Chinese provinces and cities, the word "road" being substituted for "street." The finest shops are on the Nanking Road and are situated in the first three or four blocks after leaving the Bund. The majority of these establishments, and some of them are quite extensive, belong to foreigners, although there are a few that are conducted by Chinese. The best of these is devoted to the sale of Canton goods of various kinds, such as gold and silver ware, carvings in ivory and sandal wood, embroideries, porcelains, etc.

Where the foreign portion of the Nanking Road (or Maloo, as the natives call it) ends, the Chinese shops begin. The street extends for quite a distance and leads out into the road to the Bubbling Spring, a suburb in which many of the foreign residents of Shanghai have built themselves delightful villas.

In the neighborhood of the Bubbling Spring we visited a Chinese tea house and garden one afternoon. We were the guests of some Chinese gentlemen and were the only foreigners in the place, which was thronged with men and women, who were smoking, chatting, drinking tea or eating sweetmeats. The dress of the women was in some instances quite rich, their hair arranged quite elaborately, and they seemed to delight in fanciful hairpins or other ornaments. Many of them were attended by their *amahs* or servants. Of course we could not understand a word of what they said, but their behavior was quiet and modest. On asking one of the Chinese gentlemen in our party, as to the status of the people we saw about us, we were told that none of the females were respectable; in fact, that they were all of them women of pleasure. He went on to say that, according to the custom of the country, respectable women are kept out of the sight of men; that a wife would not expect to see any man other than her father, her husband or her brother, and that when she, on rare occasions, leaves her home to pay a visit, it is always in a sedan chair or carriage with closed curtains.

Many of these women have the small feet that one reads of in all accounts of Chinese customs, but until you have seen them hobbling about with shoes of the size to fit a large doll, you fail to realize how diminutive they are. The custom obtains in the northern and central provinces. In Canton it is not followed. I asked a Chinese acquaintance of mine about it, and of course said that I thought it unnatural and absurd. He replied, " Perhaps it is so, but please remember that the ladies in Europe and America have an equally unnatural fashion of compressing their waists."

While walking in the pretty public garden a few days ago, I was joined by a young man who has been living here for some years, and who kindly gave me more or less information, with, as it turned out, some misinformation, in answer to the various questions with which I plied him.

I had been struck with the Jewish cast of features and general appearance of the Parsees whom I had seen from day to day in the pleasure ground at Shanghai, where, after the heat of the day, you may meet many of the ladies and gentlemen of the Settlement, and, in the care of their Chinese or Japanese *amahs*, a multitude of babies.

The grounds are tastefully laid out, with fine beds of pinks, roses and other flowers that thrive nicely in this warm latitude. Especially noticeable were the magnolia trees, bearing flowers some ten

or twelve inches in diameter . In the con-
servatory near by there is a fine collec-
tion of ferns and some choice orchids.

From five o'clock in the afternoon until
seven, a military band, the leader of
which is an Italian and the players from
Manilla, discourses music which is good
enough as far as choice of pieces goes, but
is quite middling as regards the quality
of the performance.

But to return to the Parsees, in whom I
had become much interested, although I
had up to that time not made the
acquaintance of any of them. I had
asked whether they have a place of worship here, for I wanted to visit one of
their temples, but was told there is none
in Shanghai. I had also been told that
they religiously abstain from the use of
tobacco, considering it a profanation of
fire. After that I watched them carefully, but never saw one of them with
either a cigar or a cigarette.

They are, as a rule, fine looking men,

with keen black eyes, aquiline noses, clear cut features, and a light olive complexion. Their faces are expressive of intelligence and self-command. All that I have seen during my walks wore the European costume, except as to the head covering, which is a peculiar sort of turban and in some cases a brimless cylinder sloping backward.

In answer to my question, my companion informed me that the Parsees are highly respected as intelligent men and honorable merchants.

"What business are they usually engaged in?"

"Some few are brokers, but the most of them deal in opium."

"Are they generally successful?"

"Certainly they are; the Jews are all rich."

"That may or may not be the case," was my reply; "but we are talking about Parsees, not Jews."

"Oh! you surprise me," he answered,

"I thought every one knew that the Jews and the Parsees are one and the same."

After that, I concluded not to pursue the subject any further.

The Public Garden, with its pretty flowers; the laughing and romping children, their elders sitting on the comfortable benches or walking along the winding paths; the music of the band; the fine view of the **Whangpoa** River, alive with shipping of all kinds, from the noble P. and O. steamer down to the *sampan* that, navigated by a half-naked boatman, glides noiselessly by and, with the eyes at its prow, really seems to know just where it is going;—all these elements combined make up something more than a picture, for they appeal to more senses than one and leave an impression that it will be both easy and pleasant to recall in future days and in less genial climes. When, as sometimes happens, the setting sun floods the western sky with a blaze of gold, or tinges the soft haze that hovers over land and water with delicate opaline hues, the scene acquires a new charm. You linger until the short twilight has dropped into black night, and forget all the kindly advice that has been given you anent malaria and Shanghai fever.

And here let me say a word about the climate of Shanghai. My experience is, of course, but limited, but the opinion I have formed is borne out by that of persons who have lived here some twenty or thirty years. With clean and temperate living, and with due regard to the precautions that we are bound to use even at home during the heated term, living at Shanghai is as healthy as in Boston, New York or Philadelphia. One of the gentlemen whom I asked about this, thus expressed himself:

'I will tell you the whole story in a few words. Young men come out here, and, being away from their families, with much idle time on their hands and little restraint in the shape of public opinion, fall into a freer mode of life than they have ever known. They eat too much, they drink too much, and perhaps commit other excesses. Finally, when they have undermined their health by these ruinous courses, they write home that the climate did it all."

The Public Garden is supported by a tax to which the Chinese contribute as well as the foreigners, but no Chinaman is permitted to set foot within its precincts, excepting of course the clever native gardener and his assistants. It seems just a little singular that the Englishman, the American, the Frenchman, the Hindoo and the Japanese can thus combine to keep John Chinaman off of this piece of ground which he has presented to them for public purposes and towards the maintenance of which he contributes a certain share. One wonders whether there ought not to be a sort of Civil Rights Bill for the protection of the native against the foreigner. When you speak of this to the

Shanghaians, you are told that if you were to admit the Chinese there would be no room for anyone else.

Two thoughts force themselves on the observer: First, that this ignoring of the native, so consistent with the policy of the foreigner in China, goes far to explain the want of sympathy between the two sections of the population and furnishes one reason for the slow growth of Western ideas and culture in this empire. Second, that the Chinese are a peaceful, docile, order-loving people is evident from the manner in which they submit to this order of things.

You have hardly entered your room at the hotel before you are called upon by the tailor, the shoemaker, the barber, and traders of various kinds, who offer their services in choice "pigeon" English. If it be known that you care for old embroideries or porcelain, you will be pestered by pedlers without number, and with some of these you may find it worth your while to deal. The price at which you eventually buy is far below that asked you in the first place; sometimes only a quarter or a third of the "asking price." Some of the embroidered pieces taken from old-time costumes show exquisitely fine workmanship and a beautiful arrangement of colors and tints.

In the native part of the Settlement one is struck by the large number of establishments for the manufacture of coffins. There are also several shops devoted to wood carving, and in some of these excellent work can be found in the way of figures or groups, illustrating national manners and customs. Driving out by the Canton Road or the Nanking Road of a hot Sunday afternoon, we found the native shops all open, and some of them seemed to be doing a thriving business. As we passed the butchers', the bakers' and the confectioners' shops, we saw the fat proprietors and their assistants naked to the waist and hard at work.

Although the *jin-ricsha* and the Chinese barrow are much used here, there seems to be a large supply of horses. The Chinese seem much given to driving out of an afternoon, and you can meet hundreds of traps and rigs of all kinds on the road to or from the Bubbling Spring tea gardens. When high dignitaries go about they use the sedan chair, which is carried by four coolies. Should it be a *taotai*, for instance, who takes an airing, his chair will be preceded and followed by a crowd of retainers, his exalted rank requiring this.

XVI. A CHINESE THEATRE, ETC.

Astor House,
Shanghai, June 20, 1887.

We are in for the rainy season, and have had rain nearly every day since our arrival. There is so much humidity in the atmosphere that, while the mercury is not very high, the weather is close and stifling. The thermometer marks between 80° and 85° F., and yet I am obliged to have a fire built in my room during the afternoon to counteract the dampness. In the mornings I find my shoes and clothing covered with damp-mould. Altogether, this is neither cheerful nor comfortable.

To-day there is much anxiety about to-morrow's weather; for the Queen's Jubilee is to be celebrated with parades and cathedral services, a garden party on the grounds of the British Consulate, and, in the evening, fireworks, a grand illumination and more parades.

On the 15th I attended the "smoking concert" of the Shanghai Literary and Debating Society, at the Lyceum Theatre, where several hundred gentlemen were assembled. I went there as the guest of Consul-General J. S. Kennedy, the President of the Society, who has been very obliging to me during my stay here. The performance consisted of songs, instrumental solos, readings and recitations, by members of the Society, and some of the numbers were very cleverly done.

Shanghai, June 26th, 1887.

After all, it rained on the 21st, and the illumination was postponed until yesterday, the 25th. There were showers at intervals through the day, and just now it looks as if it never would stop raining.

Despite the rain, the show was a great success. The crowd of Chinese that thronged the Bund was of itself a sight worth seeing, and I was at a good point to get an excellent view of the whole display, for I was stationed on the top balcony of the Shanghai Club-House. I have no doubt that to-morrow's newspaper will give a more satisfactory account of the affair than I can furnish, and I shall therefore send it to you.*

A few nights ago I visited a Chinese theatre on the Canton Road, in the Chinese portion of the foreign settlement. On our way there we passed by all sorts of shops and restaurants, kept by natives and, as usual, dirty and ill-smelling. The street looked picturesque, however, with the moving throng of *jinricshas*, chairs and pedestrians, and the gayly colored lanterns that were suspended in front of the shops and at the

---

* See Appendix.

entrance of the gate-ways between the buildings. The crowd was bustling, merry and noisy.

The theatre is quite large. In those portions of the house that we would call parquet, parquet circle and balcony, the seats are arranged in groups of four or six around tables. These are the first-class seats. In the second-class part of the theatre there are no tables. You are supplied with tea *ad libitum* and also with dried watermelon seeds, which the Chinese seem to relish greatly. They chew them and then spit them out on the floor. As smoking is encouraged, cigar stumps and cigarette ends find the same resting place. You can also purchase sweet-meats and cakes of various kinds, the waste of which is sent to keep company with the cigar stumps; and, as the floor is a Chinese one, it looks as if it had never been assaulted by a scrubbing brush.

There was acting, with and without

singing, and an exhibition of acrobatic performances. The latter were clever, intricate, grotesque and interesting. The actors were, according to Chinese custom, all males. Those who enacted the female roles dressed as women, and sang and spoke in *falsetto* voice. The costumes were rich and varied; the masks and the painted faces were excellent; but as to scenery, everything was of the crudest, hardly deserving the name.

The music was one incessant, horrid din. There was the Chinese fiddle, well played and with a tune that was quite distinguishable. But the artist who "presided at" the gong, with the unflagging assistance of the energetic and zealous performer on the tam-tam, banged away as if trying to deafen both actors and audience. If one could even understand what was being said on the stage, the music would prevent your hearing it. During the progress of the play, the Chinese gentlemen who had invited us to go to the theatre with them, obligingly translated much of what was said, thus giving us a notion of it and enabling us to judge of the quality of the acting which, to me at least, seemed quite clever. Despite the ear-splitting music, we sat through the long performance for the sake of witnessing the acrobatic battle scene, which was very near the end of the programme.

Besides handing around tea and watermelon seeds, the Chinese have a custom, at their dinners and other entertainments, of bringing you a towel, about twelve inches square, which has been dampened in hot water, and with which you are to wipe your face and hands. In a warm room this is very refreshing. The towels are handed about quite frequently. In a private house, or at a small and select entertainment, they are very acceptable and are sometimes rendered more so by a delicate perfume of one sort or another. In the theatre, however, you wonder whose face and hands they have last been used on, for the only rinsing they get is to be steeped in hot water for an instant **and** then squeezed out.

XVII. Foreigners in China—A Jewish Synagogue, Etc.

Concerning the social habits of the foreigners resident here, there is not much
to be said. They are very hospitable,
and the attentions shown a stranger usually come in the form of invitations to
tiffin or to dinner. The dining hour is
7 P.M. in winter and 7.30 P.M. to 8 P.M.
in summer. There is but little visiting
in the evenings, and social calls are
usually paid between 4 P.M. and 7 P.M.

There are many clever and interesting
people here, and a temporary sojourner
who is armed with proper letters of introduction can be sure of a pleasant time.
In that respect I have been very fortunate, and have been made welcome in
charming homes, where, aside from the

bounteous hospitality that one soon comes to look for here as a matter of course, I have met men and women inter-ested in literature and the arts, well up in all the topics of the day, and bright and clever conversationalists withal.

The houses of the foreigners are, as a rule, large; the rooms, on account of the summer heat, have high ceilings, and the furnishing and appointments suggest a blending of Western comfort with East-ern luxury. Public entertainments are few and far between, and, because of their rarity, are fairly well patronized, even when indifferent as to quality. There is an amateur orchestra, a choral society and the thriving Shanghai Liter-ary and Debating Society. For out-door sports there are cricket, lawn tennis and, of late, base ball. Horse racing and yachting also have their votaries. So, when all is told, and I suppose I do not know enough to give you more than half the story, there is variety after all in the

so-called monotony of Shanghai life. It
is easy enough to understand how the
European or American is constantly long-
ing to return to the home he has left, and
quite as easy to comprehend how, when,
after several years spent here, he goes
back to that home, he is all impatient to
return to Shanghai, where, paradoxical as
it may seem, he feels that life if narrower
is yet freer, and where he knows and is
known by every man he meets.

And now, although it is about 10 **A.M.**
in Philadelphia, I shall say good-night to
you.

Shanghai, July 7, 1887.

To-day's temperature is such as to
make it unwise to venture out of doors
until four or five o'clock in the afternoon,
and yet, sitting in my room, I am obliged
to place paper weights on the various
small articles on my table lest the **fine**
breeze should scatter them. Thus far I
have found the summer no worse than at

home, and have had nothing to complain of in the way of weather, except the long rainy spell, which lasted about three weeks, and, fortunately, ended on the 1st inst. From the second to the fifth, inclusive, we had delightful days, with cool, moonlight nights, enabling us to have a jolly celebration of the glorious Fourth, at the American Consulate. Yesterday brought us showers and enough damp mould on my clothes and bedding to render it necessary to have a fire built in my room.

On a recent Saturday I started out to find the Jewish Synagogue. It is on the Foochow Road, and not far from the Bund. I had gotten the address from the Hong Book, or directory, but when I reached the place designated, saw nothing to indicate that I was near a house of worship of any kind. I walked along a narrow paved way that suggested the entrance to a stable yard, and turning to the right saw a clean, cheerful looking house, at the door of which there sat a bright-eyed youth, who greeted me politely, and whom I asked where the Jewish Synagogue was to be found. He told me to wait a moment, ran into the house, and soon returned in company with a man about forty years of age, who informed me that the Synagogue was up-stairs, and kindly offered to show it to me. On inquiring, I found that I was addressing the *hazan* of the congregation and, in all probability, its *schamass*. He told me that he came from Jerusalem. His command of English was such that I found it easier to converse with him in German, which he spoke with an unmis-takable Polish accent.

The Synagogue is a room about thirty or forty feet square, taking up the entire upper floor of the building. It is plainly yet neatly furnished, with the portion in which the women sit railed off from the rest, in true orthodox fashion, for the Jewish community of Shanghai is too limited in numbers to indulge in the luxury of dividing itself into sects. Unless my memory is at fault, the society numbers between thirty and forty members in all, and, according to the statement of my informant, would long since have ceased to exist if it were not for the liberality of the Sassoon family.

He told me, further, that the service for the day, according to the custom during the summer months, had been held early in the morning. As it was nearly eleven o'clock when I paid my visit, I, of course, missed it.

———

I have been much interested in several young Chinamen who were among the party of students sent to the United States some years ago in order to become educated in Western science. It is well known that, owing to the influence of certain officials who were opposed to such measures of progress, and who claimed that the sole effect of sending these youth abroad to mingle with outside barbarians, would be to denationalize them, they were recalled before they had a chance to complete the course of studies prescribed for them. Three of these gentlemen, Messrs. Chu Pow Fay, Kit Foo and Tong, are stationed at Shanghai, in government employ, in the Department of Telegraphs. As a matter of course, they speak English with ease, and they are bright and clever men. I have been much in their society, and owe them thanks for their unremitting kindly attention during my stay here.

XVIII. TIENTSIN.

On board the S. S. Chung King,
Cheefoo, July 10, 1887.

Late in the afternoon of the 7th, I received a telegram summoning me to Tientsin. I at once asked Mr. B., who was to go with me, to secure passage for both of us, while I set about closing up my affairs at Shanghai. At about 7 P.M. he returned to the hotel and informed me that there were two good state-rooms to be had on this snug little steamer, and that he had engaged them. Shortly after eight o'clock, aided by one of the Chinese servants, I set about pack-ing, and at 9 P.M. I sent my luggage on board. As the steamer was not to leave until three or four o'clock in the morn-ing, we remained on shore until near midnight. When I awoke the next morning, we were steaming out of the Yang-tse, and during the greater part of that day we were in the yellow water.

We reached here at about one o'clock this morning, and for the next hour or two sleep was rendered impossible by the noise incident to the loading and discharging of freight. We expect to leave at about eight o'clock. I have been up since five, have had my bath and my cup of coffee, and, instead of going ashore for the short time at command, have concluded to remain on board and write you this letter.

Cheefoo is a small settlement on the southern shore of the Gulf of Pechili and is quite noted as a watering place. There is a fine sandy beach, or rather spit, and the sea-bathing is said to be excellent. The place is visited by foreigners as well as natives, and I have just had the country-seat of Viceroy Li Hung Chang pointed out to me.

On the first morning out from Shanghai, a big, red, jolly face looked into the
window of my cabin, with a cheery
" Good-morning, sir." I answered the
greeting, and asked, "Are you the Captain?"

" I draw the Captain's pay," was the
reply, and it of course was Captain
Hutchinson, a Scotchman from the Shet-
land Isles. I have found him agreeable
and communicative. There are only four
first-class passengers: a Mr. Ohlmer and
his wife, Mr. B. and myself. Mr. O. is a
German, who has been in the Chinese
customs service for a number of years,
and has much interesting information to
impart about China and the Chinese.

Since leaving Shanghai we have had
delightfully cool weather, fine sunsets
and beautiful moonlight nights. By to-
morrow noon we hope to reach Tientsin.
Last night it was three months since I
took leave of you at Broad Street Station.
I have almost reached the limit of my

outward journey. How soon I may be retracing my course, I cannot as yet say.

Tientsin, July 16, 1887.

On Monday morning, the 11th inst., we found ourselves approaching the Taku forts, at the mouth of the Peiho, the most corkscrew-like and the muddiest stream I have ever seen. It is all turns and bends; there are, I believe, some twenty or more between Taku and Tientsin. It is quite shallow, and its width in many places is less than the length of our steamer; so you can readily understand that it requires careful navigation to avoid running aground.

We were between five and six hours in coming the short distance. On the way we passed a number of villages, consisting of mud huts occupied by fishermen and farm laborers. Boys of various ages were running about stark naked. They were of about the same color as the muddy river in which they seemed to be very fond of swimming. In the Bay of Cheefoo I saw, for the first time, fishermen walking about on stilts, at some distance from the shore.

The country on either side of the Peiho is flat and uninteresting, but quite fertile. It is intersected by numerous canals for irrigating purposes. We saw men and women working the treadle pumps that lift the water from the river into these canals, and saw quite a number at work in the well tilled fields, and in the peach and apple orchards.

We reached Tientsin at about noon and proceeded to the Astor House, which seems to be a favorite name for hotels in this part of the world. As regards accommodations, it is rather a primitive sort of establishment, but the *cuisine* is good and the landlord is quite obliging.

The foreign settlement contains a population, all told, of about 300. As the houses and offices are generally situated in large enclosures, surrounded by high walls, this portion of the city takes up more ground than one would suppose. Thus far, I have not found it interesting, and I have already seen so much of the Chinese suburbs that I have no desire, in this very hot weather, to visit the old city, which, I learn, has from 600,000 to 800,000 inhabitants.

This is a busy port, the second in importance in the empire. Junks and steamers are stretched along the river side and the Bund is so piled up with freight, waiting shipment or just discharged, that there is but little room for pedestrians or *jin-ricshas*. During the winter months, when the Peiho is closed by ice, business is at a standstill and Tientsin is in great measure cut off from communication with the rest of the world.

I have been very kindly received by Mr. E. J. Smithers, our Consul, and by Mr. R. M. Brown, the Tientsin representative of Russell & Co. Certain business matters take up a good portion of my time during

the day; although I have a leisure hour
now and then, the heat is so excessive that
I do not feel tempted to go out of doors,
unless it be in the evening.

To celebrate the Queen's Jubilee, the
English residents of Tientsin recently
opened the Victoria Park, a large enclosure provided with a good fence and a
music pavilion, and which will some day,
I suppose, be nicely laid out with flower
beds and pretty plants, after the manner
of the Public Garden at Shanghai. In
the evenings a band of fifteen or twenty
performers, all of whom are Chinese, play
there on clarinets, cornets, trombones and
the other instruments that go to make up
a proper military band. They were
taught by an Austrian, and play marches,
polkas and other light music, quite cor-
rectly, but just like so many automata.
It was very amusing to listen to them in
a medley of negro airs, played in their
angular style and without the lilt that
one is used to.

Although I have letters to our Minister and to various other notables at Peking, I shall have to forego the visit I intended to make to the Chinese capital. To go there and return would take a full week. I cannot well spare the time, the heat deters me from making the attempt, and I am told on all sides that this is an unfavorable season of the year to visit Peking.

The streets, bridges and public buildings of Peking are described as in a state of dusty decay. I am told that the funds in the Imperial Treasury have been very low for a number of years. There is no general system of taxation. The various provinces are laid under tribute in order to support the Imperial Court and its retainers. There are said to be over 30,000 of the latter, none of whom, as they belong to the reigning family, are allowed to take positions, even in government employ, but subsist upon the bounty of the Emperor. Now, what with famines

and other causes, the provinces were, during several years, unable to contribute as
liberally as was expected of them. As a
result, the great army of dependents on
the Imperial bounty have been obliged to
manage on about a fifth or a sixth of
what they usually received. Under these
circumstances, there was no money for
public purposes.

Within the past two or three years
there has been some improvement in this
respect; and if the present promise of
large receipts in the way of tribute is
borne out, there is a fair prospect that
something may be done to improve the
roads of Peking and the general aspect
of that vast city.

XIX. THE RAILWAY PROBLEM.

If the Chinese have been more tardy than the Japanese in adopting the tele-graph, the telephone, and the railways, or in taking advantage of the great mineral wealth of their country, they have, it is claimed, at last taken up these instruments of modern progress in so thorough and effective a manner as to bid fair to dis-tance their island neighbors. They have already a system of telegraphs connecting the cities along the coast, and extending inland along the Yang-tse-Kiang as far as Hankow, and beyond. The service is as good as can be expected with the simple methods now in use, for such refinements as duplex and .quadruplex instruments have never yet been seen by the Chinese telegraph operators.

The points covered by the telegraph lines indicate the proper route of the first railways to be built, viz., southward from Peking to Canton, connecting the great cities along and near to the coast, and westward along the Yang-tse-Kiang; while lateral routes acting as feeders to these lines will open up the interior. The advantages resulting from such a system readily suggest themselves. Among the most obvious of these may be named the greater commercial prosperity of the nation, the improvement in the general condition of the population that must result from inter-communication between the inhabitants of the various sections; the means of forwarding and distributing food supplies in time to avert the famines which, in seasons of bad harvests, have decimated the population of entire provinces; and the facilities for moving and concentrating troops in order to suppress popular uprisings.

China is rich in mineral wealth. A few

mines of coal and gold have been opened. With railways these could be made more profitable and a number of others would be developed. The commerce of the coast and river ports is already considerable; with railways connecting those ports with the interior this trade would be greatly increased. By the present methods the journey from Tientsin to Peking, a distance of about eighty miles, takes about three days; with a railway it would take about three hours. During the winter months trade between Tientsin or Peking and the outer world is practically closed, because of the ice in the Peiho. All this will soon be changed. To what extent the new order of things will affect the leisurely and deliberate ways of the Chinese merchant and trader is a most interesting question, to which the future alone can furnish the answer. Time, with the Chinaman, seems to have no value. He is never in a hurry, and cannot understand why you should be. The aforesaid Chinese merchant, although well-known to be shrewd beyond comparison with his commercial rivals, bears the highest reputation for honesty, and is certainly clever enough to profit by the advantages about to be offered him.

China needs the railway for the reasons stated and for many others that will readily suggest themselves. To create such a railway system (in accordance with the government policy that railroads and mines must belong to the Chinese themselves), requires a more orderly system of finances than obtains at present. China, speaking of the eighteen provinces, presents a fine object lesson of an unfavorable phase of "states rights." The finances, if such they can be termed, of the various provinces are conducted independently, without reference to each other, and with regard to the Peking government only in so far as the annual tribute is concerned. There is no "budget" in any of them. The Viceroys, appointed by the Emperor

for three years, and holding office at his
pleasure, levy the taxes and determine
that such and such impost must yield so
much money, their object being to raise
enough to enable them to pay the required
tribute and run their own government.
There is no general tax levied by the
imperial government, and falling alike
on all subjects; indeed, there is no general
system of finance.

This accounts for the high rate of
interest paid on such loans as the government has effected.   The lowest I know of
bears $5\frac{1}{2}$ per cent.   There are others
made within the last few years paying 7,
8, and 9 per cent. respectively, although
the receipts from the imperial customs
are pledged as security.

The establishment of a national bank
has repeatedly been urged on the ground
that it would help to regulate these matters to the great advantage of the government and the people, and, although
the subject has been under consideration

for about fifteen years, it is impossible to say when, how, or by whom, such a bank will be established.

There are progressionists like the Viceroy Li Hung Chang, Marquis Tseng, and others, who clearly see that China would be benefited by the introduction of some of the results of Western civilization; but their efforts are hampered on all sides by the prejudices, and the reverence for precedent, of the large majority of those without whose consent they are powerless to act. However powerful a minister may be, he has not the privilege of independent action. Whatever he may wish to undertake must be deliberated upon with his co-adjutors, and the doubts and objections of the most obstinate must be overcome before a point is gained. This calls for great adroitness and judgment on the part of him who desires to introduce new measures. Above all things else, he must not be in a hurry. To secure the end he has in view, he must be content to make haste slowly. This is in accord with the Chinese temperament and also helps to avoid the necessity of retracing a step after it has once been taken.

That an advance has been made, and that the next decade or two will find this most conservative of nations holding quite a different position from its present one, as regards appliances for intercommunication between the various sections of the empire, is quite certain.

XX. HOMEWARD BOUND.

Grand Hotel,
Yokohama, August 7, 1887.

On the 26th of July I left Tientsin, and had great pleasure in doing so, for I cannot recall a more uncomfortable fortnight than the one I passed there. After we had gotten beyond Taku Bar, it was a great relief to be at sea once more, and I soon lost the feeling of discomfort that I had been unable to shake off while in hot and dreary Tientsin.

It was not so easy to get away, after all. I was ready to leave on the 23d. There are usually outgoing steamers on every day of the week, but at that time there were none in port, and the S. S. *Pautah*, from Shanghai, was so long overdue that fears were entertained for her safety. On the 24th a small steamer arrived, but declined to take any passengers because she had been ordered to sail in quest of the missing *Pautah*. On the 25th there was another departure, but the captain politely informed me that he had cabin accommodations for only two passengers and that he had been "bespoke" by the *taotai* of Cheefoo and his Secretary, the clever Mr. Wong-Kai-Ka. Finally, during the afternoon of that day, the S. S. *Tung Chow*, Captain Shaw, arrived, and I was informed that she would sail the next morning. I lost no time in securing passage, and, before retiring for the night, had sent my trunks on board.

I arose early on Tuesday, the 26th, for the steamer was to leave the wharf at 8 A.M., and I need not assure you that my departure from Tientsin was none the less enjoyable because of the thought that I was at last homeward bound. After a pleasant passage of about three days, I reached Shanghai, early on the morning of the 29th. On our way down the coast we saw the *Pautah*, which had run aground in a fog near the Shantung light. Our engines were stopped, and we waited while Captain Petersen, the commander of the wrecked steamer, came on board the S. S. *Tung Chow* and acquainted Captain Shaw with the particulars of the disaster. As the sea was running pretty high, it was some time before Captain Petersen's boat reached us. His crew were hard at work trying to save some of the cargo. More than half of the vessel was under water and it was becoming dangerous to remain on board much longer. Captain Shaw kindly proffered his services to Captain Petersen, who shortly afterward left us, whereupon we resumed our course.

At 5 P.M., of the 29th, the same day on which I reached Shanghai, I left there per S. S. *Tokio Maru*, Captain Wynne, for this port. We had dirty weather all the way, and reached here, thirty-six hours late, last evening. If all goes well I hope to be able to leave for San Francisco per S. S. *Belgic*, on the 13th.

———

Here my letters end. After a pleasant week in Yokohama, during which I saw much of the friends I had made during my previous stay, and renewed acquaintance with many of the sights and not a few of the curio shops of that city and Tokio, I sailed on the 13th, per S. S. *Belgic* (Captain Walker), for San Francisco, where we arrived on the 27th.

On the afternoon of the 29th I left 'Frisco, and on the 4th of September I reached Philadelphia, much the better in health and spirits for the extended trip I had taken, and all the happier at being home again.

APPENDIX.

CHINESE PIRATES.

[Philadelphia *Evening Telegraph*, May 24, 1888.]

The China steamer yesterday brought news to San Francisco of the extraordinary wreck of the costly S. S. *San Pablo*, which occurred on April 24th, on a reef off Turnabout Island, in the Formosa Straits, off the China coast. Only brief cable reports have been received of the disaster. The vessel struck a sunken rock in a thick fog early in the morning. Every one was aroused, and the Captain soon saw that the vessel must be abandoned, as she was filling fast, and showed a tendency to capsize. Just before the life-boats were ready to be lowered, a swarm of Chinese piratical junks came from the neighboring mainland. The queer-looking vessels sailed in line of battle, and Captain Reed, realizing the danger his charges were in, made preparations to repel the attack. The pirates, however, came in such numbers that before any demonstration could be made on board the sinking vessel, the pirates were climbing up the ship's sides.

They were led by a man who was armed with a cutlass and a revolver. His shipmates were also heavily armed. Captain Reed passed revolvers and guns among the passengers and crew, and after a furious fusillade the coolies were beaten off. They rallied, however, and made a second and more desperate attempt to board the *San Pablo*, which was fast settling in the water. Some of the pirates gained the main deck, in spite of the gallant stand of the passengers and crew, and were swarming towards the promenade deck, where the defenders were busy firing and reloading, when Captain Reed brought the ship's hose pipes into requisition. The long coils of hose were manned by the crew, and instantly the pirates were again put to flight, the torrents of boiling water from the pipes sweeping many of them off the decks into the sea.

The coolies then beat a retreat, and, drawing their vessels up in line, cruised half a mile off the sinking vessel, with the evident intention of waiting for the abandonment of the vessel. During the fight Captain Reed imprisoned all the Chinese among his crew with the Chinese passengers in the forehold, for fear they would aid their countrymen in the attempt to loot the vessel. As soon as possible the passengers, mails and specie were put into the *San Pablo's* small boats, and then all bore away for the mainland. When only a short distance from the wreck, Captain Reed and his charges saw the pirates set sail and rush upon the *San Pablo*, as they had done a few hours before. They clambered over the ship's sides with grappling hooks, and were soon masters of one of the finest boats that

ever sailed the Pacific. Whether by accident or de-
sign, they soon set fire to the ship, and when last seen
smoke was pouring from the wreck in great clouds.
The passengers were taken to Hong Kong, and tugs
were sent to the relief of the *San Pablo*, but they
found only the hulk, burned to the water's edge, and
stripped of everything valuable.

It is estimated that at least a score of pirates lost
their lives in this stubborn fight with Captain Reed
and his men. During the battle the women and children who were on board the *San Pablo* sought the
state-rooms, where they were in constant fear not only
of falling into the hands of the pirates, but of being
drowned in the water which was filling the ship.

The *San Pablo* was fitted up in finer style than any
steamer that ever left San Francisco, and was valued
at $500,000, which is a total loss, as she was uninsured.

HER MAJESTY'S JUBILEE.

[*North-China Herald*, of July 1, 1887.]

The hopes that were formed on Friday that Saturday would be fine were doomed to disappointment. It did not pour, and there were delusive intervals of calm, but notwithstanding the unfavorable weather the Committee decided to carry out the programme, and complete the celebration.

Undeterred by the dark clouds and intermittent drenching showers, the various bodies forming the procession began to arrive pretty punctually at the Police compound, where they were arranged in order by Mr. Drummond Hay and started about five o'clock. The streets along the route were literally packed with Chinese spectators, but the utmost good order prevailed, and there was no interruption to the progress of the procession through the dense crowd. Indeed, the quiet demeanor and orderly conduct of a Chinese crowd upon such occasions strike a foreigner very forcibly and favorably. Despite of the dispiriting surroundings the processionists made a very brave show.

*   *   *   *   *

The windows of the houses along the way were

crowded with delighted spectators. The appearance
of the procession marching along the gayly decorated
Bund was particularly effective, and all that it wanted
to complete the beauty of the scene was a more
smiling sky overhead. The band of the *Braun-
schweig* was meanwhile discoursing its best music in
the grounds of the British Consulate, where the garden
party had commenced under the sadly depressing
influences of drenching rain and a sward converted
into a marsh.

The garden party could not by the most unblushing
optimist be pronounced a success. But the fault was
entirely upon the shoulders of the Clerk of the
Weather, an official who had for days been trifling
with the Committee and driving them to the verge of
desperation. The hospitality of the hosts—the whole
British community in general—was lavishly extended
to the visitors who came, if not in their thousands in
response to the general invitation, at least to the number
of several hundreds. The large marquées were filled
with refreshments in solid and liquid form, a pretty
novelty in the shape of Japanese day fireworks was
introduced, and gave much amusement, and the hosts
and the guests combined to ignore the efforts which
the elements were making to damp their spirits. It
was decidedly a garden party under a cloud, dripping
trees, and on a quagmire, but, even so, it was enjoyed
to a certain extent. The Consular offices had all been
turned into reception rooms, with tables laid out for

refreshments, and in these and the verandas troops of ladies found shelter from the rain.

*   *   *   *   *   *   *   *   *

At eight o'clock the work of lighting the thousands of lanterns which were strung the whole length of the Bund, and on all the houses, was begun. The Japanese lanterns, which were hung in festoons across the Bund at frequent intervals, had all succumbed to the weather, dropping down in dozens, the eager *jin-ricsha* men rushing at them as they fell, and laying in a fine supply of candles for future use. But the indomitable energy of Mr. Gratton was not to be conquered even by this *contretemps*. Fresh strings of lanterns were brought up, lighted and swung from the tops of the masts, and by nine o'clock, when all the illuminations, with one notable exception, were alight, the river front of Shanghai, from one end of the harbor to the other, presented a sight which it has never shown before, and is not likely to again, until the Jubilee of Shanghai itself comes round. Indeed, there are not many cities in the world where such a *coup d'œil* as was obtained from the houses on the Bund, could be got, the great bend in the river lending itself admirably to the display. Countless thousands of lanterns of all colors were alight in an almost continuous line of some three miles. The river, too, was lighted up. The men-of-war were covered with lanterns from the trucks to the rails, but there was nothing prettier than the illumination of the P. & O. S. S. *Ravenna*, whose masts, yards, funnel and mizzen trysail were outlined in fire, until she looked like a phantom ship studded with yellow diamonds; and in every port along her side shone a lamp. Far down in the harbor was a large river paddle steamer whose whole outline, paddle-boxes and all, were traced out in fire. There was hardly a ship or steamer or yacht that was not hung with lanterns, and the darkness of the night, with the heavy canopy of clouds, from which rain fell occasionally, aided the effect. Punctually at nine the preparatory gun sounded from the *Sapphire*, and at the same moment the yard-arms and other points on the *Ravenna* were illuminated with blue-lights, which also blazed up from the men-of-war. From these and from the pontoons in the river, the upward shower of rockets now began, to the accompanying roar of the vast crowd of Chinese, who braved the inclemency of the weather. It would be impossible in reasonable limits to describe all the illuminations.

* * * * * * * * *

At nine everything began to go at once. At three points on the foreshore the Canton fireworks were being displayed, and the set pieces were watched with the most intense admiration. Fire balloons went up at intervals and rockets continuously, and the effect of the latter was very curious. The clouds were so low and thick, that the rockets nearly all disappeared. Then there was a gleam of light in the cloud as the rocket burst, the colored stars coming back into sight, like meteors, after an appreciable interval.

THE DRESS OF JAPANESE LADIES.

[*The Times*, London.]

A number of eminent American ladies, headed by Mrs. Cleveland and Mrs. Garfield, have addressed an open letter "to Japanese women who are adopting foreign dress." The writers say that as Japan is rapidly taking rank with other nations of the earth in all that pertains to Western civilization, it is not strange that foreign innovations have at last reached woman and her attire. If the ladies of Japan have made up their minds to adopt Western female dress in its entirety it would be useless to urge them not to do so, but the writers of the letter are anxious that they should first know that those who have studied the subject hold that there is great need of improvement in certain particulars. From the standpoint of beauty, grace and suitability (the letter goes on), Japanese dress, modelled after the best Japanese standards, is both elegant and refined, and it would take years for Japanese ladies to adapt to themselves and wear with equal grace a costume to which they are entirely unaccustomed. As to economy, European dress, with its ample skirts and trimmings, requires a large amount of material, and even if native stuffs are used the expense of the costume will be greatly increased, to say nothing of the change and expenditure in household furniture necessary if Western dress be adopted. Foreign carpets, chairs and tables must be added to foreign dress and shoes, and Japanese household interiors, now held up to the world as models of grace, simplicity and harmony, will have to be entirely remodelled. But it is to the relations of foreign dress to health that the attention of Japanese ladies is especially directed. Heavy skirts, dangerously close-fitting dress bodies, "the insidious custom of wearing corsets, far more direful in its consequences than the Chinese custom of compressing the feet of women," are all commented on. Some of the writers think that the charge of immodesty sometimes made against the present Japanese dress could be met by the addition of underclothing. All these observations are made "that Japanese ladies may be made aware of the dangers in such a course before adopting foreign dress, and that they may be led to stop and consider well before doing what will affect, not only their own health, but that of their sons and daughters."